G000016637

TYRANNY
AND THE LASH

TYRANNY AND THE LASH

PRISONERS AND
PUNISHMENTS IN
BRITISH HISTORY

Stephen Wade

ROBERT HALE · LONDON

© Stephen Wade 2011
First published in Great Britain 2011

ISBN 978-0-7090-9244-5

Robert Hale Limited
Clerkenwell House
Clerkenwell Green
London EC1R 0HT

www.halebooks.com

A catalogue record for this book is available from the British Library

2 4 6 8 10 9 7 5 3 1

Typeset by Eurodesign
Printed in the UK by MPG Books Group Ltd, Bodmin and King's Lynn

CONTENTS

INTRODUCTION

We begin with two scenes from the criminal justice system as it was in British history 200 years ago – with the first being a glimpse of what a 'civilized' nation was capable of in the Regency period.

Some of the most notorious cases of women being tried for wilful murder in English history involve moral beliefs and ideologies of power that are impossible to accept today. Something profound in the human mind and in the sense of moral community feels an extraordinary revolt at the thought of a woman taking the life of another. Until 1827, if a woman took the life of her husband, she was not committing murder, but petty treason, and that meant, up to 1790, a punishment of burning at the stake, not being hanged. When a woman was hanged for husband murder, even as late as 1825 the ritual in the official execution was very different from that of a male killer. This account from *The Times*, 9 August 1825, of the death of Hannah Read, demonstrates this:

> A bed or mattress was placed upon the sledge, which was drawn by a horse, upon which the prisoner was secured by a rope. On reaching the bridewell, she was carried into the prisoner's house…About eleven o'clock she was again placed upon the sledge, and was drawn along the prison yard to the foot of the steps leading to the scaffold; soon after she appeared on the platform followed by the High Sheriff and

the usual attendants...She seemed earnest in supplicating mercy for her sins and invoking the divine favour on her unfortunate children and relatives...

Hannah Read had a very different experience from that of the average male murderer. Her crime was also a more extreme form of sin and a more outrageous offence against the existing social and religious hierarchy.

The second example concerns a teenager in 1859. In that year, Harehills Lane in Leeds was mainly rural. The fields there were a pleasant place to walk, and in that particular August an old man who lived in Roundhay, Richard Broughton, decided to take a leisurely walk into the city. There was a path that began north of the city and followed mainly what is today the Wetherby Road near Seacroft down to Oakwood and into Harehills. He did not have much on him that might attract robbers – just a florin and his watch. But he was set upon by two men who beat him severely about the face and skull, and stole the watch. Amazingly, the old man staggered to his feet and, after some men and a young boy had come to his aid, he was guided northwards, and walked back home.

He was very severely injured, but a doctor was called and the police went to look at the scene of the crime. Broughton died not long after, so the search was on for the killers. The victim had tried to describe them: one was young and the other quite a lot older. Two suspects were found: Bearder and Appleby had been in prison for another crime, but the police asked around and witnesses, particularly at a pawnshop where the victim's watch was pawned, were asked to identify them. But the evidence was not clear-cut and there was an alibi for Bearder.

The hunt then went towards Castleford, as a man called Smales had bought a pawn ticket for the watch, and was collared when in the shop. The Castleford connection led to Charles Normington, and gradually evidence was gathered that put him in the picture as the major suspect. He had repeatedly tried to sell the pawn ticket, and that meant that lots of people recalled him over the period of days that the police were looking at for movements related to the murder.

Normington was arrested in Sheffield; he was only seventeen. In custody he kept trying to fabricate a story, then finally claimed that another man had killed Broughton. But the finger still pointed at Normington and he was tried in York in December. The defence was that he was merely an accessory, and that the man with him committed the murder. But details concerning the young man's bloodied shirt counteracted the argument. The death sentence was passed, and Normington's mother, who was present in court, screamed loudly. After the sentence, Normington broke down and confessed to the murder.

This was before the abolition of public hanging, and 10,000 people turned out to watch a teenager die on the scaffold. One newspaper report noted: 'When the child-like figure appeared, the crowd were instinctively hushed and remained so until the execution was complete. They dispersed in silence and shame, their heads bowed…'

Since Victorian times, the British have always been troubled by questions of what prison is for and whether or not it works. Before that, the dominant view of a prison was that it was where one sent the 'underclass' and those who transgressed. That sounds very simple, but in fact it is much more complex, because those who broke the law were not all violent and dangerous types who would slit your throat as soon as look at you. Many unfortunates were debtors, victims of hard justice or incompetent lawyers, but at the heart of our prison history is a story of neglect and oblivion.

Until the eighteenth-century Enlightenment thinkers, there was very little thought given to the mass of people crammed into the prisons across the land. Throughout the Medieval period, prisons were the province of local power bases, civil, military and ecclesiastical; later, after the creation of the first house of correction at Bridewell in London (hence the later generic term, 'bridewell') in 1555, these prisons became business concerns, funded from local rates but existing to make a profit from convict labour.

The horror of the prison was primarily the prospect of death from prison fever: the early assize records list thousands of names of prisoners who died in prison while waiting the assize trial – that is, people awaiting trial. The history of our prisons is inextricably linked to the growth of the assize court system and the story of the assize courts is a reflection of how criminal law gradually developed and found a system that would have parity across the land. The courts represent the boldest step by which central legal power began to cover the king's domains, using the local and the national elements together. In each shire, the sheriff, who had been there since very early times, gathered the jury and the other machinery of law, ready for the visit of the assize judges, because that is what assizes were – courts done in transit – giving the assize towns distinguished visitors and a high level of ritual and importance for a few days each year.

Originally, the law courts followed the king, and his own court was the *Curia Regis*. Then in Magna Carta (1215) there was this sentence: 'Common pleas shall not follow our Court but shall be held in some certain place.' The result was that Westminster was made that 'place', but eventually the notion of having top judges moving around to deal with criminal and civil cases became a workable option, with economic and logistical benefits of course, as persons accused would be retained and then tried mostly in their own counties or provinces.

Since early Medieval times, there had been assizes – literally 'sittings together' – to try causes and to gather officials in the English regions to compile enquiries and inventories into local possessions and actions. These were 'eyres' of assize, but they were not courts. The assize courts came when travelling justices went out into the counties to try cases: the Assize of Clarendon in 1166 and the Council of Northampton in 1196 decreed that the country should be split into six areas in which the judges of the High Court would sit. These became known as circuits.

In Edward I's reign an Act was passed to create court hearings in the local place of jury trial, before a summons for the jury to go to Westminster. The people involved were to come to London unless the trial had occurred before: in Latin, *nisi prius* (unless before). What developed over the centuries was that serious offences, crimes needing an *indictment*, had to be tried before a jury. The less serious offences, summary ones, could be tried by a magistrate. In addition to that, the terms *felony* and *misdemeanour* also existed until they were abolished in 1967: a felony was a crime in which guilt would mean a forfeiture of possessions and land, so the offender's children would lose their inheritance. A misdemeanour was a less serious crime. Prison sentences were therefore very different: felonies resulted in death, transportation, or long sentences of hard labour.

The justices of assize had a number of powers. First, they had a commission of *oyer and terminer* (to listen and to act) on serious cases such as treason, murder, and any crime that was labelled a felony. They also had to try all people who had been charged and who had been languishing in prison since their arrest, and they tried cases *nisi prius*. Basically, the judges would hear and sort out the cases relating to those languishing in prison.

The assize circuits became established as the Home, Midland, Norfolk, Oxford, Eastern, Western and Northern, and the records for these run from 1558 to either 1864 or 1876 when assizes were reorganized, or to 1971, when the assizes were abolished and crown courts created. From the beginning, the assize circuits covered all counties except Cheshire, Durham, Lancashire and Middlesex, with the first three being referred to as the Palatinate Courts. In 1876, some courts moved from one circuit to another.

The result of all this means that a criminal who committed a crime in Leeds, for instance, after 1876, would be tried in Leeds rather than in York, the former seat of an assize for the West Riding. The assizes were held twice a year from the thirteenth century, until they ended in 1971, and these sessions were referred to as Spring and Winter. A third session could be held at times if the prisons were full – as in times of popular revolt and riots, or activities by gangs.

Court business was divided into two areas: for civil cases – referred to as 'crown' – and criminal cases. Two judges would be on the road, each with a responsibility for one of the two areas of law. In the law reports in *The Times*, these are clearly marked in capitals. For instance, for the Winter assizes in York in December 1844, we have:

> # WINTER ASSIZES
> ## NORTHERN CIRCUIT
> ## YORK, DECEMBER 5.
> (Before Mr Justice Coleridge)

The newspapers tend to use the terms 'crown side' and 'criminal side'. The judges arrived, and the hearings took place: the long line of prisoners, in irons, would stand before their learned lords, and some would be freed, some would be sent back to prison, and some would be sentenced to hang.

The poor person waiting for trial could be sitting for months in a bug-infested, smelly and infected dark space, sometimes in irons and often on a starvation diet. The prison fever was so extreme that it was common for judges, lawyers and anyone else in court to catch the fatal disease from the person in the dock. Deaths were regularly announced in the journals and periodicals; on several occasions, hundreds of men in the army died through prison fever infection after one of their number rejoined the force after a spell in prison.

The first real attempt to make the public aware of this terrible state of affairs was made by John Howard, a county sheriff and landowner who took upon himself the task of visiting the prisons across the land. The result was his book *The State of the Prisons* (1777), which provides the kind of material we might expect in an official report, mixed with documentary insights. It is clear from Howard's writing that the local prisons and houses of correction were so determined on making a profit that they rarely considered the kinds of topics we discuss today with regard to prison life: how first-time offenders and juveniles might be corrupted by old lags; how mental illness and deprivation mean that a prison is a place of care as well as of retribution, and how staff should have some kind of training for this special work.

After Howard, it still took a very long time for significant change to come: a major report of 1818 and a series of reports on prisons published in *The Gentleman's Magazine* in 1805–7 made it clear to everyone that statutes meant to reform and improve prison administration were just not working. Abuses were rife; sinecures were easy to obtain and, above all, the exploitation of convicts as cheap labour was indicative of the attitudes of most administrators. It took very significant events to effect change, and the first signs of improvement came with Sir Robert Peel's Gaol Acts of the 1820s. Boroughs had always had lock-ups, and small local prisons had been used for short-term imprisonment, but it was gradually coming to be seen that a new kind of prison was needed. The penitentiary arrived at the same time as the Prison Acts were used to try to establish inspections and better-quality security and care.

Unfortunately, the penitentiary notion was not the general cure-all in penology that many imagined. The failure of the first one at Millbank signalled future problems for anything done on a very large scale. It then became recognized that a national system was needed, but that was not to come about until 1877. In the fifty years between Peel's Acts and the nationalization of prisons, there were still profound problems, largely as a result of poor administration, repressive regimes and inept governors. Transportation to Australia came in 1788 and lasted until the 1850s, and was meant to remedy the crime wave across the land, and the consequent problems of overcrowded prisons. Unfortunately, it led to the use of prison ships – 'hulks' – and high death rates on board ship, followed by harsh regimes in the prison colonies.

In the twentieth century, after rationalization and closures of smaller prisons, specialist establishments began, first with the Borstal system and then by more specialized women's prisons and a more refined system of categorization of prisoners according to the level of perceived risk to the public in each case. Today, problems of overcrowding are still there, and levels of mental ill health in the prison population are still high, but administration is advanced and the impact of criminology has had a deep effect, as efforts to improve rehabilitation have increased.

In spite of progress and change in ideologies and applications of new ideas, the media-generated images of prison history still tend to be dominated by cruelty, suffering and vicious punishment. The Georgian and Victorian years provide the social contexts for these images. The facts support the view that a person in a British prison in the years before *c.* 1900 was in for a very hard time indeed, both mentally and physically. A glance at some statistics and examples will support this view. Between 1750 and 1772, for example, on the Midland Circuit of the assizes, 1,057 prisoners were transported and 518 were condemned to death, although 116 of these were actually hanged. In terms of deaths in prison, the figures for 1559–1625 on the Home Circuit represent a typical profile: between 1562 and 1579 in one prison alone – Colchester – thirty-seven prisoners died of prison fever.

Tyranny and the Lash sets out to tell the stories of the prisoners, staff and governors over the centuries, from the dungeons to the convict prisons, and from the massive penitentiaries to the Victorian radial prisons and the Borstals. The saga of repression and punishment in that history presents every kind of human cruelty: the regimes depended on instilling fear and on forcing mental torment. Among the following tales there are accounts of vicious applications of the cat o' nine tails, people crammed into solitary cells, poor inmates reduced to skeletons in their lice-ridden straw beds, and arrogant amoral governors and keepers who pushed for profit at the expense of human life.

Timeline of Prison History and Punishment

1115   The first true prison on record: the baulk house at Winchester.

1165   Bedford prison established.

1166   The Assize of Clarendon directed that where there are no prisons, sheriffs are to construct them.

1275   Statute of Westminster.

1332   Hexham prison completed and opened.

1361   The first justices of the peace.

1423   The first version of Newgate prison erected, funded by Richard Whittington.

1450   First recorded use of the Tower rack.

1485   The Court of Star Chamber created.

1534   Treason Act (building on the 1351 Act).

1555   The first house of correction established, at Bridewell, Blackfriars.

1576   An Act to establish houses of correction across the land.

1597   An Act for establishing workhouses for the poor was passed.

1686   Last hanging for witchcraft in England – that of Alice Molland.

1714   Vagrancy Act: first statute to provide for the detention of lunatics.

1735   The Witchcraft Act repeals the death penalty for witchcraft.

1744   The Madhouse Act: made licences for private madhouses in the London area.

John Howard published *The State of the Prisons*, a survey and critique of all local prisons.

The arrival of the first fleet of transported convicts in Botany Bay.

1790   Abolition of burning of women in England for petty treason.

Jeremy Bentham proposes his idea for a penitentiary.

1800   Criminal Lunatics Act: medical supervision made a legal requirement.

The Select Committee on Penitentiary Houses recommends a penitentiary be built at Millbank (the current site of the Tate Modern).

Abolition of beheading.

1817   The last recorded public flogging of a woman in England.

The flogging of women prisoners is abolished.

1830s   The 'Silent System' introduced.

Abolition of dissection after hanging.

1834   Abolition of gibbeting in England.

The Millbank experiment fails: the prison is closed.

The first recommendation that hanging is done in private, inside the walls.

The Carnarvon Committee recommends a regime more attuned to punishment.

1863   Broadmoor opened as Broadmoor Criminal Lunatic Asylum.

The end of convict transportation.

Hanging is made private.

1879   Abolition of branding as a punishment.

The Departmental Committee on Prisons indicates that there should be another switch of emphasis, from a stress on punishment to an investment in rehabilitation.

The crank and the treadwheel were finally abolished.

The establishment of a Court of Criminal Appeal. The first professional probation service created.

The Borstal Act establishes the first juvenile offenders scheme with the new ideas of a standardized regime in place.

This was for people aged between sixteen and twenty-one.

1917 Dartmoor prison receives over a thousand 'conscientious objectors'.

1932 Mutiny at Dartmoor prison.

1946 A serious mutiny at Northallerton prison.

1948 Military drill introduced at detention centres.

1976 Serious riot at HMP Hull.

1983 Charles Bronson stages a rooftop protest at Broadmoor.

1990 Riots at Dartmoor prison.

1991 The Criminal Justice Act: 'integral sanitation' introduced. In other words, 'slopping out' ended.

Ronnie Kray dies.

1999 Charles Bronson takes an education officer hostage at HMP Hull.

Reggie Kray is released from prison on compassionate grounds, and dies a few weeks after release.

2007 'The Istanbul Statement' – this puts forward the guideline that solitary confinement should be prohibited for death row prisoners and life-sentenced prisoners, for mentally ill prisoners and those aged under eighteen.

1

DUNGEONS AND OBLIVION

The period 1100–1500 saw massive changes in English law. The process of dealing with criminals moved from a reliance on local courts run by the manorial lords to the assize circuits – courts controlled by travelling justices working on behalf of the 'King's Peace' in his realm. Before the Norman Conquest in 1066 when William of Normandy ('The Conqueror') began the long line of Plantagenet sovereigns, the Saxon communities had worked by 'hundred courts' and 'Frankpledge'. This meant that a small local group, led by a responsible elder or elders, would take responsibility for hearing accusations and applying punishment. By 1500 there had been a gradual evolution of statute law, with clear notions of trial and punishment. The jury had been created and justices of the peace ran the local and regional hearings.

All this was an amazing achievement. For the Germanic Anglo-Saxons, an assortment of laws had been listed and defined by the kings of various areas or shires. These relied on trial by ordeal or combat. Punishment was seen as a sliding scale depending on the nature of the transgression. King Ethelbert of Kent had decreed, for instance, that a murderer would have to pay a hundred shillings, but if the victim only had a facial bone smashed, then the fine would be twenty shillings.

The Church was a powerful influence on criminal law and penalties were handed out for offences such as fornication, eating meat during a fast, or doing a deal with the Devil. There was a strong tradition of both the Church and the state taking fines rather than punishment, as the kings were always in need of more cash in their coffers. After Augustine landed at Thanet in 597, the Church developed its own grand ideas of compensation: if goods were stolen from a holy place, then the bishop was entitled to twelve times the value.

Particular injuries to people also involved compensation from the assailant with a similar rationale. An eye was valued at fifty shillings, a toe at six pence, and if a thumb was damaged such that it had to be cut off, then twenty shillings had to be paid.

There was nothing universal here: different rulers had their own ideas of punishments. The worst destiny for a villain in many ways was outlawry. An outlaw was a man who had been placed outside the protection of the law. A male aged over fourteen could be outlawed, and criminal *indictments* for treason, rebellion, conspiracy and other serious *felonies* could lead to a criminal outlawry. In civil courts, a man could be outlawed for severe debt problems.

Because both the Church and the state had notions of legislation, the concept of sin was gradually absorbed into the common law. Serious crimes such as murder, rape and robbery were *torts* (wrongs) but then later were definitely sins, so there had to be penance, as in the murder of Thomas à Becket and Henry II's long-lasting penance as he took responsibility. But generally there was an increase in severity and brutality in punishments until the first proper criminal law measures of Edward I in the thirteenth century.

We know the word 'posse' from Westerns in which a group of men were gathered by the sheriff to help him chase and catch the robbers. In Medieval England there was a sheriff (from the word 'shire-reeve') and he was responsible for all kinds of regional legal work. One of his jobs was to assemble a *posse comitatus* to pursue the rogues on his patch. This was a group of people from the community who saw that pursuit and retribution was their task. There was also the hue and cry – the general alarm and call for help if a crime was committed.

As night-time was the most dangerous time, when families and citizens were most vulnerable, there was the concept of 'watch and ward' – the gates of walled towns being shut, and the 'watch' was responsible for that work.

Edward I (1272–1307) earned his nickname, 'the English Justinian', after the emperor who codified law in the later Roman Empire. Edward created the Statute of Westminster in 1275, a legal code intended to reduce the abuse of the legal system by the people within it. He also enlarged the powers of the sheriffs and 'keepers of the peace' who were to become the first 'justices of the peace' in an Act of 1361. In the Anglo-Saxon period there had been a *tithingman* – a person responsible for this 'hundred' of people, and the justice of the peace inherited that role, but on a larger scale.

In a Yorkshire parish in 1310, Sir John Elland murdered members of the rival Beaumont family so he could have their land, yet no one was destined for a spell in prison. A reading of the court rolls and assize records for the fourteenth and fifteenth centuries gives a clear impression of the attitudes at the time towards crimes of violence. Murder, rape and serious assault were rife. In 1451, a gang of 400 armed men went into the quarter sessions at Walsingham in Norfolk and took out their friends who stood accused. In 1348 in Yorkshire, there were eighty-eight cases of murder on record. One writer has calculated that today that proportion of killings in the population would mean that there would be around 10,000 murders a year. The assize rolls contain hundreds of cases in which a man has abducted a neighbour's wife or entered a home and raped the women, and simply had to pay a fine. Only rarely did such criminals go to prison.

Looking at the Medieval period through modern eyes, it is hard to imagine the complex structures of the authority of both crown and Church in all areas of an individual's life and death in that Catholic universe. The higher clergy had a significant level of personal status and sway among their flock, and the wealth of the Church went along with this. Of course, they had their own courts and prisons as well, and their provinces were centres of great influence. A story from York shows the power of the Church as prison and gallows owner.

The old Ainsty area of York was integral to the Benedictine Priory at Micklegate, and the priory of Holy Trinity was a powerful establishment, with rights given to it by the king, reaching back to Henry I.

One of those rights was the power over criminals who were apprehended within the Ainsty; this meant that such persons could be hanged in the area, and there was a Priory scaffold. King Stephen had granted land to the Priory, and as the gallows stood there, it was known for some time as 'the thieves' gallows'. This chronicle of hangings begins with what is arguably the strangest of all the tales, because in fact he survived the hanging.

The man in question was John Ellenstreng. All we know about his offence is that he was 'convicted of larcenies' and so sentenced to hang; he was a member of the Guild of the Hospital of St John of Jerusalem, and luckily for him, his fellow monks were allowed to take away the bodies of any of their number who had dangled from the

LEMAN REDE, YORK CASTLE, 1829

Frontispiece from Leman Rede's book of trials, which contains accounts of the prison experience for those convicted at York assizes during the late eighteenth century.

scaffold. They came for him, to give him a Christian burial, and when they arrived at their chapel (St James on the Mount), to their amazement John was still breathing. As was usually the case in the Medieval centuries, myths were generated from this, maintaining that he had been saved by blessed intervention – that St James himself had saved John's life.

The man who had been 'hanged' on 18 August 1280 was given a pardon later by the king himself, following a written account of the strange event by a witness called John de Vallibus, who was one of the justices in the Eyre (circuit court) of York.

The story shows that prisons were made whenever and wherever they were needed in the period before the eighteenth century when houses of correction were developed along with local prisons. Between 1165 and 1500 there were eighty local prisons built by county sheriffs and funded from rates, in addition to houses of correction. Yet that is only part of the story of prisons in the Medieval and Reformation period. The Church had prisons, and manorial courts needed them also, as they had their own offenders to deal with at times, and this was no easy task, as another York story, the one below, shows.

Thomas Wilson was charged with the murder of one George de Walton, who was the abbot of St Mary's; the abbot was just one of the victims of Wilson (who in fact used two names – Wilson and Mountain), who entered the church of St Peter's to wreak murderous havoc on 13 July 1300. Wilson also stabbed another clergyman, the Right Reverend Father in God, Edmund Grindal. It was to be a long trial, lasting four days, but the real drama came afterwards, in the prison.

Wilson was found guilty and sentenced to death. He was put in the hell-hole of St Peter's prison to languish until the day of his death, but he was wily enough to almost escape. He tried more than once to scrape and cut his way out, at one time using a piece of plate he had managed to shape into a cutting-tool. The desperate man made a hole through a brick partition and somehow managed to move into the gallery of the chapel, even with a weight of fifty pounds in fetters strapped to his body. The condemned man worked through a thinner partition and ended up under the roof of the building but, unfortunately for him, his movements were heard and he was recaptured. Wilson/Mountain was eventually hanged at the gallows of the Abbey of St Mary at Clifton.

At York there were always problems with the gaolers being bribed and helping prisoners to escape. The gaolers were also fond of extracting money from prisoners, it seems. In 1388 a commission was formed to bring to justice the York gaoler, William Holgate, issued by the sheriff of Yorkshire, John Saville. Holgate was accused of

> permitting divers felons therein to escape, and compelled other prisoners by duress and divers penalties to become approvers [informers] and to appeal lieges of the King of felony, whom he caused to be taken and detained in the said prison, he extorting sums of money from them and withdrawing the alms given for their maintenance.

Holgate soon joined his charges behind bars.

Medieval prisons as custodial places – temporary locations for people awaiting trial – are linked mainly to the status of the sheriff, as he was responsible for bringing an alleged criminal to trial. After the Assize of Clarendon in 1166, periods of prison confinement become more common. Many prisoners were detained for committing a felony, for treason or for forest offences. In addition, debtors began to be detained by the marshal until a trial concluded. In the thirteenth and fourteenth centuries, sheriffs, marshals and others committed people to the Fleet or Tower prisons in London. Most prisoners did not, as famous people did in the Tower, dine with the constable and have a comfortable bed. Most prisons were sheriffs' prisons, and the stories of prisons across the land, together with the dozens of London prisons established since Newgate (from 1423) and the Marshalsea (eleventh century), are mostly of common people.

The county prisons probably had few gaolers until the twelfth century, when such people are mentioned in pipe rolls; prisons were in castles or elsewhere within a borough and the sheriff ran them, being completely in control. But by around 1280 the word 'prison' had a wide range of meanings. By that time there were the national prisons in London, the county prisons and the franchise prisons. The latter were owned by clerics or barons, and of course these began employing keepers and gaolers. As for the prisoners, the fact is that much of the time there was anarchy, and barons and their gangs could abduct and imprison victims, as in this account from this Bill put to the king for legal action:

> William Piers of Brompton complains to the justices of our Lord the King that whereas he was going in the peace of God to the town of Ludlow on the Sunday next before the feast of St Michael, Roger Clayband, Reynold of Posenhall…Together with all the commonalty of the town of Ludlow…came and suddenly attacked him with swords…and wounded him in the head and stripped off his hose…and they dragged him off to prison and there they kept him for two days and two nights and put him in shackles, wrongfully and against the peace…

This was a fairly common event; the court rolls of the Medieval period are full of violent assaults, rapes and killings, and abduction. In many cases fines rather than prison sentences were given, but in the county prisons, for those who did find themselves imprisoned, what happened to them? If they were hostages, state prisoners or prisoners of war they were maintained from the Exchequer. But for common criminals, suspected felons, they had to fend for themselves: in prison, they had to somehow fund their upkeep from their land and chattels. One man hanged for murder in 1228 had possession valued at thirteen shillings, and the sheriff was allowed to take four shillings from that – as payment owed for sustenance we assume.

Debtors had a very hard time, but at least, by the Statute of Acton Burnell of 1283, they had to be given bread and water by their creditors if they were destitute. The dark side of prison life at the time is seen, though, in a case from York in 1295. The eyre (trial) was in session and a large number of people were to be tried, but the business was suspended as there was a war in progress against the Welsh. The waiting prisoners were returned to prison and forgotten. The account

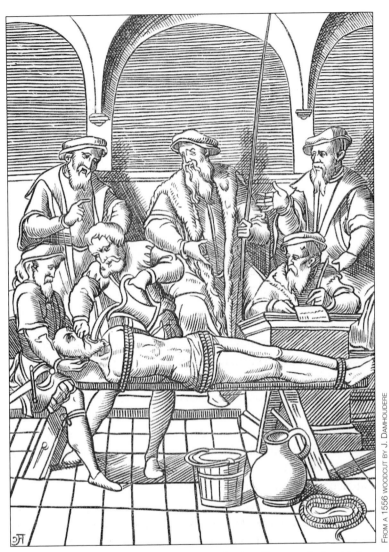

FROM A 1556 WOODCUT BY J. DAMHOUDERE

Water torture – one of the most barbaric forms of torture. It was applied mainly to those accused of treason.

of the miserable consequences of this states that 'a great multitude' died in prison, having starved to death and, as an emergency measure, a special prison delivery session was held to prevent more deaths.

Of all the prison tales of the years before 1600, surely the chronicle of the Star Chamber and the Fleet provides the worst examples of maltreatment. The Star Chamber was a special court, established in the reign of Henry VII; its brief was to deal with serious offences in its own way, outside the usual courts of law. It had a right to apply special penal jurisdiction, and so it was useful to such extreme characters as Sir Thomas Wolsey who needed to try and punish the more powerful opponents they had against them. Sir Thomas Smith said it was there to 'bridle such stout noblemen or gentlemen who would offer wrong by force to any manner of men...'

The Star Chamber had no jury and it could use torture. It could also issue a death penalty. It was ideal, later on, as an instrument of tyranny for the king, and those sentenced by that court generally went to the Fleet prison. By 1600 it was seen as the best place to send troublemakers, as defined by the king. It was on the Fleet river, running into the Thames, and was astride a polluted stretch. One resident described it as a 'noisome prison, whose pestilent airs are not unlike to bring some alteration of health' – a massive understatement. Prisoners had somehow to pay their fees for lodging and food. Prisoners were attacked, sexually assaulted, robbed and placed where they would suffer from cold and deprivation. There was even a fee to be paid to avoid being shackled in irons. There were dungeons in the lowest reaches of this hellish place, for those who were, in effect, sentenced to die by the powerful keeper.

In 1691 Moses Pitt published his account of life as a prisoner in the Fleet, called *The Cry of the Oppressed*. Of all the horrendous injustices the Fleet prisoner suffered was the law by which a creditor of a debtor in that prison could have a writ of *habeas corpus* which would force the debtor to be transferred to any other prison. It is a writ directed at anybody who has another in his custody, ordering the person to be placed before a judge.

Pitt was at one time a rich man. He rented a printing house from the Bishop of Oxford and he produced a well-rated atlas and several

Bibles. But he started speculating in property development and built a magnificent house in Duke Street; however, he had borrowed and the creditors came down on him – so his destiny was the Fleet.

He tells the story of a surgeon from Liverpool who also went into the Fleet, and he was so neglected and starving that he robbed a cat of its mice in order to hang on to life. When he complained about the treatment by his gaolers, he was put in irons.

In the years between the death of Queen Elizabeth I in 1603 and the accession of Queen Anne in 1702, the story of crime in England is crowded with high-profile treason trials, violent rebellions and, above all, the execution of King Charles I in 1649. That judicial killing opens up the debate about who was 'criminal' in that terrible event. It was a brutal, vicious century, with a Civil War in the middle years in which brother fought brother on the battlefield and that saw the horrendous persecutions of witches in many areas of the land.

But the famous and infamous were not the only victims of the repressive criminal law: in the year that King Charles was beheaded, twenty-three men and one woman were hanged at Tyburn (which was where Marble Arch now stands) for burglary and robbery. It took eight carts to carry the felons to their date with the rope, and the event was the largest number of criminals ever hanged in one session in Britain. The hangings were excuses for heavy drinking and violence in the London mob.

It is in the seventeenth century that the beginnings of the proliferation of capital crimes began, and these were applied to several areas of life. In the Game Laws of 1684, for instance, the taking of game by anyone except the owner of the land was forbidden. A series of statutes established this. Only people who owned a freehold estate worth £100 a year, or a leasehold of £150 a year, were allowed to take game. Poaching had always been looked upon, in rural communities, as a 'social crime' – meaning that there was a certain degree of tolerance in that often the killing of rabbits or birds might hold off starvation for a poor man's family. The thinking behind these tough laws may be seen in the 1671 Coventry Act, which made it a criminal offence to loiter with intent to maim. Sir John Coventry had been attacked and had his nose slit in London, and that prompted the legislation of course.

In terms of the political life, serious offences were punished by hanging, drawing and quartering. In October 1660, two unfortunates, John Cooke and Hugh Peters, suffered this fate: 'When Mr Cooke was cut down and brought to be quartered, one they called Colonel Turner called that he might see it…The hangman came to him smeared in blood.' He had done the unenviable task of cutting the bodies of the men in quarters while they still breathed.

The 'Bloody Assizes' of 1685 typify this savage reprisal for treason and rebellion: after the Monmouth rebellion in June of that year, in which the Duke of Monmouth had landed with an army at Lyme in Dorset, gathered a large force and proclaimed himself king, there was a brutal reprisal waiting him after his defeat. The so-called Bloody Assizes sentenced over three hundred people to death. One of the victims was seventy-year-old Lady Alice Lyle who was beheaded for treason at Winchester, convicted for harbouring traitors.

Opposing the sovereigns was always courageous and often suicidal. The great parliamentarian John Hampden opposed Charles I's demands for ship money and was imprisoned in 1627, for fighting the notion of a 'forced loan'. The great judge Sir Richard Hutton also refused to accept the legality of the Ship Money extortion by the king, but he escaped any punishment.

But for most people in Britain at this time, the common offences of daily life were dealt with in quarter sessions before magistrates, and at church or manorial courts. The records for these are primarily in Latin in this period – until 1733. But the records are not necessarily all in the county archives. Many have been printed and translated. For instance, the Yorkshire Archaeological Society printed the quarter sessions for the West Riding in parts of this century, and these give a valuable insight into the process of law.

In 1637, for instance, Sir Francis Wortley and other dignitaries sat in judgement at Doncaster on a variety of accused persons. At the end of the session, we had this situation:

> They were led to the bar by the sheriff and asked what they could say
> for themselves, why they should not have judgement of death
> according to the law for the felonies aforesaid whereof they were
> convicted. They severally said that they were clerks and prayed for the
> benefit of clergy…

The 'benefit of clergy' was the one way to escape hanging up until the
nineteenth century. If a person could recite the 'neck verse' – the
opening of the 51st psalm ('Have mercy upon me, O God, according
to Thy loving kindness: according to the multitude of Thy tender
mercies blot out my transgressions') – they would not hang, but have
their thumb branded instead. The benefit of clergy could only be
given once, and was abolished in 1827 by the Criminal Justice Act;
before this, all felonies were capital offences unless benefit of clergy
was a factor. As stated earlier, a *felony* was any offence that resulted
in the person forfeiting all land and goods to the Crown and being
sentenced to death.

But there was always the communal, public retribution for what
might be called 'moral crimes'. In 1619 there was a case in the Court
of Star Chamber in which William and Margaret Cripple of Burton-
on-Trent prosecuted residents there: they had been attacked by a
mob for 'sexual incontinency'. Not only were they dragged through
the streets, they were then put in the stocks and people 'pissed on
their heads'.

Overall, the prisons of the Medieval to seventeenth centuries were
a mix of various categories of places, all poorly regulated, and existing
either for short-term prisoners or for the everyday criminal class as
seen and sentenced at assizes or at county quarter sessions. Assize
records often give a fair reflection of the consequences of actions with
regard to the person's fate in prison. In 1645, a certain Richard Harris
refused to be tried. He was pressed to death in prison (see page 133).
Thomas Smyth and Michael Jackson, guilty of being 'sturdy beggars',
were 'branded with the letter R on their backs and delivered'.
Andrew Briscoe was to be kept in prison until the next delivery on a
felony charge.

The point about prison in Britain up to the Georgian years is that it reflects the general abuse of power and the repressive statute law, along with the ad hoc measures taken to repress sedition, treason and any upstart regional force that might be a threat to the status quo. Until the proliferation of capital crimes created in the eighteenth century, and the numerous Acts relating to crimes against property and person, prisons were not under successful regulation and were run by people who were mostly content to hold rather than to care.

2

SOLITARY, FEVER AND NEGLECT

By the seventeenth century the prisons and bridewells across the land had become places where all kinds of people were crammed together beyond society and left to rot. Only the wealthy, fallen foul of debtors, could enjoy a reasonably comfortable life behind prison walls, because they could buy food and drink from the traders who came into the prisons. Generally, dumped into prisons were felons, debtors, small-time thieves, prostitutes, beggars and invalids. They were the last residence of what society considered to be trash.

On 2 January 1752 an anonymous prisoner wrote this letter to the *Gentleman's Magazine*:

Mr Urban,
I am an unhappy prisoner now lying in one of the prisons within this kingdom, to which I was committed about 10 months past, on an accusation of felony, though entirely innocent as afterwards appeared on my trial, my poverty and want of friends preventing any person till then from speaking the truth in my favour. But the grievance I complain of is not my commitment for a crime of which I was not guilty, but the tyranny and oppression of the prisoner, for after I had been declared innocent by the jury, and the prosecution found to be on malice and ill-nature, instead of being immediately discharged, I was hurried back to the prison again, there to lie till I could raise 30s

to pay the prisoner what he calls his fees. If any situation on earth merits pity or any evil merits the attention of the legislature, surely 'tis the case of unhappy prisoners in my circumstances. I have lain here six months, my family starving, my credit and character ruined and my spirits broken, without any means of procuring redress against the unjust prosecutor or any satisfaction for the numerous calamities he has brought upon me. I have heard much talk of the equity of our laws but surely if they had not been defective or abused, I should not now suffer.

Put in modern parlance, this wretched man had been on remand, guilty of no crime, and yet had been totally ruined in every aspect of his life and health. What we think of as 'remand' at that time was awaiting prison delivery if at assizes, or some other kind of trial in other courts, and there were dozens of different courts across the land in 1750, from manorial to admiralty and from military to assizes.

As the writer of this letter pointed out, the basic problem was that gaolers in local prisons rarely had no fee. From the earliest local prisons there had been sporadic fees paid in some prisons, but there was no national or regional system of fees. The prisoner or turnkey had to exist by taking a number of fees from their prisoners. This was known as 'garnish' in the argot of the time, and everyone suffered, perhaps most of all the debtors, as the writer explains as he ends his letter to the editor:

If gaolers do not have large salaries for the execution of their office, let the public pay them and let not the sufferings of the wretched be increased by their rapine...My companions here are debtors, who though they have either satisfied or been forgiven by their creditors cannot obtain their liberty till Mr Prisoner is paid his fees. Here therefore they languish, many of them with cold and hunger and some with infirmity and disease till death sets them free without fee or reward.

Debtors had a hard time. Many were middle-class professional men, such as John Wesley's father, Samuel. Today, a walk around the interior of Lincoln Castle and its prison buildings gives little idea of what the Georgian prison would have looked like. But part of that prison remains, built by the great John Carr, who worked on the exterior. Inside, it was designed by William Lumby, a Lincolnshire man. In that inner sanctum would have been the governor, his relatives, and the debtors of the county. In 1705, one of the inhabitants of that awful place was Samuel, then rector of Epworth in the Isle of Ancholme.

This fact might come as a shock to some, as it is easy to imagine the country life of a local churchman as being peaceful and comfortable, as he would receive plenty of local help, and would have his own plot of land (his glebe) on which to keep pigs or hens, or even grow vegetables. Samuel did have some of these things, but the problem was that he made enemies in his own parish, and these were so fierce and intractable that they virtually ruined him.

Both Samuel and his wife Susannah had blood links with nobility, and Samuel's Dissenter roots had brought him a good education and useful contacts. He aspired to write and to travel, and was always full of plans and schemes on a grand scale; at one time he seriously put forward a career move that involved disseminating religious knowledge and faith in India. He was always looking out for a more comfortable income, as his family was large; but he had a knack of making enemies. In his first living, at Ormsby in south Lincolnshire, he had offended John Sheffield, Earl of Musgrave, by throwing the peer's mistress out of the rectory when she was making a social call.

When the Wesleys moved to Epworth, Susannah had just had her sixth child; it was going to be hard, and Samuel took an extra living, bringing in the nearby village of Wroot. But Samuel's awkward, unyielding and argumentative nature even caused a split between man and wife: Susannah would not say 'amen' after a prayer to the king and Samuel sulked, sleeping in another room. This was the man who was to find that not only his nature, but sheer bad luck, were to strike at him, despite his efforts to make progress in the world. Susannah, known as 'Sukey', was the daughter of the great scholar Samuel Annesley of London: she knew her doctrine and her Bible, but she also stuck to her principles. It was a marriage of two strong temperaments.

One of Samuel's actions that was clearly intended to find favour in an age of patronage was a poem in praise of Master Godolphin, a folio pamphlet, and this got him noticed by the powerful faction of the Duke of Marlborough, the champion of the Battle of Blenheim. Not only was Samuel made a chaplain of a regiment for this, but he was also promised a prebend (a payment from the cathedral ruling body making him a canon); but both of these were to be lost in the terrible acrimony and vengeance wreaked on him after a political mistake.

Samuel's ruin started when he changed allegiances at a local election, first promising to support the representatives of the Dissenters, but then changing to support the church party when he learned of the aggressive attitudes of the Dissenters towards the Church. When the electioneering and news of the rector's perceived turncoat decisions reached the Isle of Axholme, Samuel Wesley was in for a very hard time. It was when he was visiting Lincoln that he first had a scent of trouble to come. As he talked to a friend in the Castle Yard, Samuel was told that his own parishioners were hunting for him, and that one had said they would 'squeeze his guts out' if they found him. After this, a campaign of terror was launched against Wesley and his growing family in Epworth.

It started with a mob outside the rectory and pistols being fired; his children were, understandably, very frightened. Samuel was then arrested for debt, initially for a sum of around £30; his flax at home was burned, the door of the rectory damaged, and his cows stabbed. There he was, locked up in Lincoln Castle, writing letters home, knowing that his own family were being half-starved and terrorized. In a letter, he gives an account of the arrest:

On Friday last, when I had been christening a child at Epworth, I was arrested in my churchyard by one who had been my servant, and gathered my tithe last year, at the suit of one of Mr Whichcott's friends…the sum was not £30; but it was as good as five hundred. Now, they knew the burning of my flax, my London journey, and their throwing me out of my regiment had both sunk my credit and exhausted my money.

Yet even in the prison, Samuel kept busy and pressed ahead with good work. He writes about reading prayers twice a day and preaching on Sunday. He was as sociable as ever, 'getting to know' his 'prison-birds' as he put it, and writing to the Society for Promoting Christian Knowledge for some books to give away. The working of the law was simple and inflexible: a debtor stayed in prison until the debt was paid. But most men in Samuel's situation would have no hope of clearing the debt; at least he had some powerful allies. Making himself busy helping the less fortunate was indeed a charitable thing to do, as many of the poorer debtors would be there for very long periods, and some would be in irons. Things had not changed much by 1776, when the prison reformer John Howard noted that 60 per cent of prisoners in England's prisons were debtors.

The most horrendous experience of the whole sorry time must surely be the desperately tragic events of Wednesday, 30 May 1705, when a mob came to the rectory, firing guns and drumming in the 'rough music' tradition of English culture, under the window where Susannah had given birth just a few weeks before. Samuel had taken the child to a neighbouring woman who acted as nurse. But this nurse lay over the baby and suffocated it in her sleep. When she woke up and found the corpse, she panicked and ran, screaming with fear, to Wesley and gave the baby to his servants. The end of this agonizing event comes with the dead baby being given to its mother. As Samuel reported it, the child was given to her 'before she was well awake', thrown 'cold and dead' into her arms.

Samuel's debts totalled £300, a very large sum at that time. He wrote about his problems to Archbishop Sharpe of York, and that good man helped him, both with money and with petitioning for help. Samuel was in the prison for approximately six months, after a Mr Hoar paid him £95 and the archbishop added more. Back in Epworth he learned how his wife had survived; she had sent him her wedding ring while he was imprisoned, and he had sent it back, but somehow she fed the family and kept morale high enough to carry on. She had had no money at all, and the food was mostly the bread and milk yielded from her glebe. But the poor man with a sickly wife and eight children had pulled through.

The prisons were limbos of neglect, with a range of punishments in the tough regimes maintained by the tyrants who held the keys and the food supplies. A few humanitarians occasionally tried to change things, but one additional problem was that offices and responsibilities of all kinds were up for sale, in an age of nepotism and corruption. The Georgian period and Regency era were times in which sinecures were bought and sold as a matter of everyday business. A publication called *The Red Book* listed these offices and their value. A typical example was the wardenship of the Cinque Ports, which paid £1,000 a year. A celebrated case was that of Ashley Cowper, younger brother of William Cowper, who was a barrister in 1723. He was also a Mason and a member of the Horn Lodge; Ashley acquired the post of Clerk to the Parliaments, a very well-paid and esteemed position. The post was in fact bought for him by his father, who just happened to be Judge Spence Cowper.

There was no investigation into nepotism and sinecures until 1780. The situation was, as Blake Pinnell has explained, that 'The law courts, the established church, part of the army and the royal household contained many positions in which the occupants did very little for the money they received.'

In the management of prison, this was a very dangerous and destructive practice, particularly as the man who bought the governorship could stay away from the prison as often as he liked, and leave a minion in charge. One of the very worst of these abuses was highlighted in the case of John Huggins, warden of the Fleet prison, who was tried at the Old Bailey in 1729 for the murder of one of his charges, Edward Arne.

Huggins bought the wardenship of the Fleet for the huge sum of £5,000 for himself and his son. Of course he then had to get the investment back, by any means possible. The Fleet was at that time mainly a debtors' prison, and we know what it was like because the great reformer John Howard reported on it. At that time, debtors' prisons had two sides: Common and the Master's. On the latter side lived those who could afford to rent their accommodation, but the Common Side, as Howard describes, was horrendous:

The apartments for the Common-side debtors are only part of the right wing…Besides the cellar there are four floors. On each floor is a room about twenty five feet square, with a fire-place; and on the sides seven closets or cabins to sleep in. Such of the prisoners who swear in court or before a commissioner that they cannot subsist without charity, have the donations which are sent to the prison, and the begging box and grate.

The grate was the street-level aperture from which they could beg passers-by for alms or even water. But their situation would have normally been like that of the anonymous writer to the *Gentleman's Magazine*, were it not for the fact that John Huggins and his gang of assistants were sadists. At the basis of the sentence was the table of fees for the gaolers: these included fees for the chaplain, the porter, the chamberlain, the turnkey; and added to that were fees for 'liberty of the house and irons when first coming in' and a dismission fee.

William Wiseman being buried after dying in prison. He was a case study in the noble deaths of recusants.

The total cost of all these fees was supposed to be under £2, but in fact £3 5s was the sum taken, as increments were applied.

Huggins decided, as he aged, that he would sell his position to a certain Thomas Bambridge, his deputy, along with another scoundrel called Dougal Cuthbert. A barbaric and murderous regime was to follow, and the scandal broke not long after Bambridge took over control. At the centre of the affair was the death of a prisoner, Edward Arne, who had been committed to a horrible den called the strong room where he starved and was submitted to infections and diseases so extreme that he lost his wits before dying a miserable death inside the walls. At the trial, the strong room was described by a witness called Bigrave:

> *Solicitor-General:* What do you know of the building the strong room?
> *Bigrave:* When I came there, there was a stable which was converted into a strong room…
> *Solicitor-General:* What sort of a place is it?
> *Bigrave:* It is arched like a wine vault, built of brick and mortar.
> *Solicitor-General:* What are the dimensions?
> *Bigrave:* It is eight feet wide and eleven feet long.
> *Solicitor-General:* How near was the dung-hill to it?
> *Bigrave:* The dunghill was as nigh as to the other part of the court.

Another witness called Bishop said, referring to Arne, 'When he was brought in he was in good condition of health and in his senses…being put in the strong room in the Fleet would have killed anybody, and that forwarded Arne's death.'

Poor Arne's last days were pitiable. A turnkey called Farringdon gave the most touching account of the man's death:

> …he grew somewhat disordered and from the time he was put in the strong room he altered every day, grew hoarse, and at last could not speak, and he grew weaker and weaker every day; about the beginning

of October he lost his voice, he then grew delirious, and ripped open his bed, and crept into the feathers, and one day he came to chapel with excrement and feathers sticking to him like a magpie, being forced to ease nature in that place…After that I saw the prisoner at the bar looking into the strong room, the door being open, and Arne was lying in the bed ripped open…

The trial was widely reported and brought into the public eye the lamentable state of the debtors in His Majesty's prisons. The story of Huggins and Bambridge gradually came out in full, as witnesses were examined. Huggins had left Bambridge to take over, before actually selling him the office of warden, but Huggins had stayed at home, miles out of London, and had only been to the Fleet twice over a period of nine months. He had left the prison in the control of a cruel, heartless monster who only wanted the profit, and was only too happy to see the prisoners die if they could not pay his fees.

How many people were in the local prisons in the years before any kind of real reform? Who were they and what do their crimes tell us about society generally at that time? The report of 1818 provides some figures. In that year there were 73,363 prisoners committed, and the number the prisons were capable of holding was 14,925. The courts often tried hard to reduce the committals, as this entry from the Guildhall shows: 'The same day the sessions ended, when 18 convicts received judgements of death; one was ordered to be transported, nine to be imprisoned…eight to be whipped and 25 discharged by proclamation.'

A few examples of the criminals admitted to prisons gives a glimpse of the trajectories of criminals, from life circumstances to offence:

M.M., a girl of 8 years of age, was found in solitary confinement in one of the prisons in the metropolis. She had been committed for one month, on a charge of child-stealing. It appeared the parents had driven the girl into the streets to beg…

A. RITCHIE, A SHORT HISTORY OF NEWGATE PRISON, 1866

This is the cover of a popular history of Newgate prison, which details the prisoners' lives.

S.M., aged 18, committed to Cold Bath Fields prison for pawning a watch, which she had taken from a house of ill-fame where she lived.

J.B., aged 13, having associated with some bad girls, was enticed from her parents in London, after being absent some time taken up at Maidstone, and committed to the Bridewell as a vagrant, being in a destitute condition...

But there were occasionally some success stories:

W.R., aged 15, committed to Newgate, tried, and discharged without any means of procuring a meal or a night's lodging. After being placed a short time in the temporary refuge, the Committee procured his admission into the refuge for the Destitute, where he remained fourteen months; his conduct was satisfactory and he has since been out to the Cape of Good Hope, and apprenticed to a respectable farmer there.

In the houses of correction matters could be as hard as the local prisons; the late eighteenth century saw several new ones being created, and they were basically businesses, often run by families from the locality. Their regime was a round of hard physical work, some levels of separation, prayer and basic education, with an array of punishments, mainly the use of the 'refractory cell' – which was a bleak form of solitary confinement.

Typical of these new establishments was Northallerton in north Yorkshire. We know a great deal about the prison from its inception in the late eighteenth century through to its radical development between 1848 and 1852 as it had to cope with far too many prisoners to accommodate with safety. It can boast that it was the first custom-built prison in England still in the prison service. That means that if we leave castle prisons out of the reckoning, the foundation for Northallerton prison in 1783 is significant in the history of penal records.

As with all county local prisons, there were many facilities existing before that date in order that the justices had somewhere to send felons as well as debtors. The site for the prison was on waste ground to the east of Zetland Street, granted by the Bishop of Durham, John Egerton. The proviso was that his bishop's court should be held there as well as the local courts for summary offences and the magistrates' court to deal with felons. One of the town's first historians, Ingledew, explains that the land was low and swampy; it contained the town rubbish dump and a pinfold – the area where stray cattle were impounded from the common land.

Dr Neild, writing in 1802, has left us a description of the house of correction:

> This prison for the North Riding is removed from Thirsk and has been built for about 20 years. The Sessions House under which are the jailers apartments adjoins. The whole is nearly enclosed by a boundary wall. The building has a double front and each has a spacious and airy court so that the sexes are completely separate.

There was a vegetable garden and a wash house; then for prisoners there were twelve cells around four yards square and divided from one another by a passage two yards wide. It is notable that two of the cells were solitary: this means that the notion of the 'refractory cells' was there from an early date. Often called dark cells, these were tiny places that were one of the key elements in the later conception of prisons as places of a punitive regime, before the nationalization of prisons in 1877. Men could be placed in these cells for days or even weeks in a space just 12 feet by 5 feet 6 inches by 12 feet high or, in the worst instance of all, a cell that was only 7 feet by 5 feet 6 inches and 11 feet high.

The place also had a large workroom (used as a chapel on Sundays) and another workroom of quite a large size. On the upper storey were the cells for women and the 'bell room' where the turnkey lived. There were five cells for women.

By 1800 it had been changed further: because there was a court-house within, a large area was made outside and there were jury rooms and magistrates' rooms added. It was long overdue; in earlier years there had been sessions held at the Guild Hall (which became the town workhouse by 1800) and then at Vine House from 1720.

The new house of correction was not ready to receive its first prisoners until 1788. In 1777 the prison reformer John Howard had published his seminal work *The State of the Prisons* and, although it happened slowly, there was pressure for reform at the local level. The first prisoners at the new venue were taken there from Thirsk; they were coming to a prison that was to be a 'going concern' as well as a prison. It was to be controlled by a committee of visiting justices who would inspect and present their reports to the quarter sessions. From their minutes we can glean very interesting information, such as this entry from 1788:

> Ordered that sacks be made of Harden [a fabric made from flax or hemp] to be filled with straw for bedding to fit the bedsteads of the different cells according to the pattern already made by Thomas Winspear. That a blanket and rug be provided for each of the beds according to the pattern produced by John Marshall.

The prisoners in this early period usually arrived in a state of dishevelment and often disease; they desperately needed new clothes, and from the very beginning a standard issue of garments was prepared: men were to wear a jacket, waistcoat, trousers and cap, the order specifying 'the right side to be made of blue kersey stuff and the left side of the same sort of material of a brown drab colour'. The women wore a jacket and petticoat, again mixing blue and drab. Comfort was not the main concern: kersey was a coarse cloth, usually ribbed; drab was simply undyed cloth, employed so often that it became a 'colour' in its own right, used by all kinds of working people.

One of the real problems was in health and accommodation; the 1837 report brought to light many aspects of the prison regime which were undoubtedly cruel and severe, though with rather perverted 'good intentions' behind them. For instance, there was no heating in the cells and there was poor drainage; although a surgeon attended the prisoners every day, he struggled to treat the constant problems of rheumatism, lung infections and diarrhoea. There were also periodic bouts of typhus fever. There was also the barbaric practice of the 'dark cells' for misbehaviour. The surgeon told the inspector, 'I do not approve of putting men in the refractory cells in the ground floor in this damp situation. I think the cells should be warmed. I have great difficulties in preserving health.' There was scurvy too, and sometimes dysentery, resulting in death.

There is a remarkable example of one prisoner who proved intractable to discipline and refused food, even in the dark cell. This man spent fifteen days in the two sizes of refractory cells over a period between 25 March and 12 May and took no food in the time incarcerated. The surgeon reported that the man was 'of a melancholic temperament and...would have starved himself to death if not released'. Everyone did their best to entice the man to eat, including the chaplain, the surgeon, the magistrates and the turnkeys, but all to no avail.

Every offence and complaint had to be logged, as always in prison administration; a typical record of this is the following:

> *Wardsman* complains of...taking a piece of oakum to tie his shirt sleeves and making a noise with the tins in the mess room.
> *Culprit*: I had no buttons, but got them from the wardsman afterwards.
> *Governor*: Care not to offend again.

In 1999 an extraordinary record book of offences heard at Langbaurgh West division petty sessions turned up in a house clearance in Hurworth. It was labelled 'conviction book no 1' and this document gives us a rare insight into the punishments meted out for less serious crimes in the community; with these punishments being backed, no wonder that cases in magistrates' courts and quarter sessions entailed such extreme sentences. For instance, in 1832 John Duffy was given two months in Northallerton for 'being an idle and disorderly person' and Robert Graham was given a month's prison for 'a wilful and malicious trespass' which was in fact throwing another man's plank of wood on to a fire.

In the local area generally there was a Society for the Prosecution of Felons. This was a trend across many parts of the land, reflecting the constant fears of the landed citizens and wealthy in terms of the threat of petty crime around them. Their handbill of 1802 expressed their concerns:

> We, whose names are hereunto subscribed, having entered into an association for the prosecution of felons...DO HEREBY GIVE NOTICE that any person who shall commit any robbery, felony, theft or larceny upon the persons or property of any of the members of the said association will henceforth be immediately prosecuted and brought to justice...

There were also physical punishments in the prison; a whip handle was used, and it was almost a foot long; there were also lashes given out by a whipcord of 21 inches. This was a period in which soldiers in the army were regularly whipped, offenders who disturbed the morality of a community were often pilloried, and in which conformity in all areas of life was expected on pain of violent repression. In Northallerton in 1820, over a one-year period, there were fifty-four solitary confinements for talking and seventy-nine confinements for other offences; there were in total 798 punishments from a prison population of 326.

The prison fever was always there, and matters did not improve in spite of a string of statutes and enquiries. A Bill of 1784, for instance, the Prison and House of Correction Bill, set out to direct justices (who controlled the administration and collected rates) 'to adopt such plans as will provide distinct and separate places of confinement, and dry and airy cells in which the several persons may be confined'. But nothing changed in most places for decades. An enquiry of 1820 reported that out of a total of 518 prisons in the United Kingdom, only twenty-three were classed as divided according to law (by the 1784 Act). The commissioners added:

> 59 prisons had no division whatever to divide females from males...In like manner, the law directs that materials for work shall be provided, and the prisoners constantly employed, but in 445 prisons no work of

any description had been introduced…many prisons are described as being in the most deplorable condition…

The bad management, neglect of legal requirements and the fever meant that charity was the only possible help for the likes of Arne or the poor man who wrote to the *Gentleman's Magazine*. Groups such as the Society for the Relief of Persons Imprisoned for Small Debts, based in the Strand, constantly appealed for donations, and listed their benefactors – such as 'Miss W', who gave two guineas in 1787, and the Earl of Hertford, who donated the huge sum of £20.

Solitary confinement was central to the running of the prisons. The germ of this punishment lies in the gradual switch from a

N O T E S

ON A VISIT MADE TO SOME OF

THE PRISONS

IN

Scotland

AND

The North of England,

IN COMPANY WITH

ELIZABETH FRY;

WITH SOME GENERAL OBSERVATIONS ON THE
SUBJECT OF PRISON DISCIPLINE.

By JOSEPH JOHN GURNEY.

SECOND EDITION.

LONDON:

PRINTED FOR
ARCHIBALD CONSTABLE AND CO., EDINBURGH;
LONGMAN, HURST, REES, ORME, AND BROWN,
JOHN AND ARTHUR ARCH,
AND HURST, ROBINSON, AND COMPANY, LONDON.

1819.

The title page of one of John Gurney's inspection tours, printed in 1819. This was one of a succession of prison inspections carried out between 1808 and 1820, during the crusade for prison reform.

constant application of physical punishment to one of deprivation. By the 1820s the notion lay behind the latest concepts of rehabilitation, but in the local prisons that Howard saw, we have a good idea of how the refractory cells were used. The prison registers at Maidstone show a typical range of cases. J. Savage was confined to a dark cell for three days 'persuant to the order of the visiting magistrate' and 'Confined to dark cell for three days, Mary Burrell, on the report from the matron that she had used improper language respecting the chaplain and for riotous conduct.' At the same prison in 1821, William Constable and George Merchant were confined in dark cells, Constable for assaulting and beating James Styles, Merchant for 'singing in his sleeping cell'.

A survey of some instances of the application of solitary confinement in the years between c.1790 and 1830 shows that it was a controversial topic, but was generally accepted as the most severe punishment except for the lash. Some of the sentences given in court specified solitary rather than the usual prison regime, as in the case of John Webb in 1828, who was in court for stealing three pewter pots from a pub in St James's. A female servant testified against him, and Webb, from the dock, took off a nailed shoe and violently threw it at her, striking her on the arm. The judge said that such an action deserved 'the heaviest penalty of the law' and that meant imprisonment in Newgate for six months, the whole of which was to be spent in solitary, and then that was to be followed by seven years of transportation.

Clearly, solitary confinement, though a regular short-term punishment in local prisons, was a special case in the general actions taken in sentencing. In 1816, William Price was sentenced at the West Sussex quarter sessions to six months' solitary confinement on bread and water for stealing a leaden weight. It was also seen as an essential punishment for young criminals, with the attitude that it would deter them from further transgression. In 1831 at the Thames Police Court, an eleven-year-old girl called Isabella Brown was charged with stealing property from her employer in Commercial Road. The girl's mother begged the magistrates to do something to 'check the girl's propensity for pilfering' and the sentence was fourteen days in the house of correction to be spent in solitary confinement.

There were some voices of dissent and some were troubled by the idea of the 'dark cell'. In 1827 at the Surrey Asylum for the Reformation of Discharged Prisoners there was a committee meeting at which this interchange took place:

> ...an objection was placed by Mr Hedger to having persons placed in solitary confinement, conceiving the punishment too great. This mode of dealing with delinquents was stated to be very efficacious, and those who entered the Society had the rules read to them before they were admitted...The honorary secretary said that at the Hoxton Institution, solitary confinement for offenders had done a great deal of good. It was at length agreed to, instead of using the words 'solitary confinement', 'separated from other inmates' should be substituted.

This classic example of euphemism and double-think would have been ridiculous to the area of society in which solitary confinement was used most barbarically: in the army. In all the annals of corporal punishment in British imprisonment, arguably the most repulsive and savage use of solitary confinement was that described by an officer of the Royal Marines in a letter to the press in 1832. It concerns a private in the Royal North Lincolnshire Militia who, in 1804, struck at his sergeant-major with the butt end of his musket. At a court-martial he was sentenced to 1,000 lashes and three months in solitary confinement in the black-hole of the main guardhouse. He was given the first 500 lashes and drummed out of the regiment.

Within the main prison estate, it was only at coroners' inquests that abuse and maltreatment of offenders came to public notice and, as is the same today, such an inquest involves an explanation of penal punishment. In 1825 at the notorious Millbank penitentiary, a young man called Lewis Abrahams hanged himself in his cell after what was alleged to have been ill treatment, including time in solitary. The governor, Chapman, had to explain what his punishment regime was, and everything was examined, from the dietary to the small comforts allowed. The coroner asked what punishments were applied and Chapman said:

There are three sorts…the first and slightest is by taking away dinner and substituting bread and water; the next is confinement in a refractory cell into which the light is admitted by a very small window and the third and heaviest is confinement in a dark cell, and bread and water…I can only continue these three days…

Lewis, it was alleged by friends, had been murdered, and that the penitentiary was like the Spanish Inquisition. Lewis had not worked properly and had refused to use the crank in the way it should have been used: this was the machine affixed to the cell wall that had to be turned so many times a day. Then there followed irreverent conduct in the chapel. The governor had kept a journal and noted all infringements done by the young man. The last in a long list was that he was insolent to his officer and was sent to the dark cell. The young man was later found in his cell, dead, after throttling himself with part of the net from his hammock.

All this happened in spite of the reports and enquiries in the early nineteenth century, and of John Howard's monumental book referred

WILLIAM SCRUTON, PEN AND PENCIL PICTURES OF OLD BRADFORD, 1890

John Nelson in solitary confinement. Nelson was a Methodist preacher who was jailed before being forced to join the army as a result of displeasing the Vicar of Birstall.

to earlier in which he made all the problems absolutely clear. On the topic of the prison fever he was direct and shocking, pointing out that from his own observations in the years between 1773 and 1775, he was fully convinced that 'many more prisoners were destroyed by it than were put to death by all the public executions in the kingdom' and he noted that there was on record an assize held at Oxford in 1577 in which all who were present died within forty-eight hours. At Taunton in 1730 'some prisoners who were brought there from Ilchester prison infected the court and Lord Chief Baron Pengelly, Sir James Sheppard, John Piggot, sheriff and some hundreds besides died of the prison distemper...'

A typical example of Howard's reporting on health issues as he went across the land and saw every prison he could find, is this from Cambridge:

> In the spring, seventeen women were confined in the daytime and some of them at night in this room, which has no fire-place or sewer. This made it extremely offensive, and occasioned a fever or sickness among them which alarmed the Vice-Chancellor who ordered all of them to be discharged. Two or three died within two days...

Some of the stories involving the prison fever from the Georgian years are heart-rending in the extreme. A man called Burt, for example, was convicted of forgery in 1790. He refused a pardon when offered one and was determined to hang because, he said, of a 'disappointment in love'. But he then won the lady over, and she came to see him in prison, where she caught the fever and died. His life of adventure continued, because he was transported to Sydney, but while on board ship he wrote to a barrister he knew in Lincoln's Inn to inform him of a conspiracy being hatched on the ship. He was taken into the captain's cabin for protection. In Australia he managed to start life again.

Howard had his own recommendations for improvement. He believed that washing and fresh air were essential and that a small stream running near the courtyard pump would help. He recalled that he had known of prisoners supposed dead from the fever, and about to be buried, being washed down with cold water, and then recovering, much to the shock and trauma of the layers-out.

There was also the other aspect of dangers to health that often caught the notice of writers and politicians: smallpox. This disease was rife in the prisons of course, and in society generally. Lady Mary Wortley Montagu, the wife of an English diplomat, was a victim, scarred by its ravages, and in England, long before Edward Jenner demonstrated the use of inoculation, she had her own daughter inoculated, and such first steps encouraged medical men of her time to experiment. Some used Newgate prisoners as guinea pigs for experiments. The man who introduced the vaccine into England was Charles Maitland, and he devised the prison tests. The king agreed that the prisoners who agreed to have smallpox engrafted on them would be freed if they recovered. The man who actually went into the prison to perform the test was Dr Terry of Enfield, who had worked on similar tests in Turkey.

Inoculations were done on six condemned men and they all recovered. The next stage was that one of the recovered men was sent to Hertford prison where it was known that the illness was rife, and there the man was to lie in bed with a sufferer. The prisoner was not affected, so that was a great encouragement to the doctors. More trials were then conducted on charity children in the parish of St James.

Smallpox was not eradicated until 1977, and it was a problem in prisons through the nineteenth century as well. As late as 1893 there was an outbreak at Hull prison and at Gateshead workhouse at the same time.

Through the years between the early local prisons to the major changes effected in late Victorian times, that fatal mix of infection, refractory cells and sheer neglect led to a very high death rate in the prisons. In spite of all the fine words and earnest reflections by the middle classes, imbued with notions of charity and equality from Enlightenment thinking, the prisons across the country were still punishing with barbaric measures. While Howard's book was at the press, in Maidstone, Mary Wheatley was publicly whipped on her back till her body was bloody, and if a typical outcome of an Old

Bailey session were inspected to see the barbarism at work, it would be this law report from 1732:

> The sessions ended at the Old Bailey when 7 malefactors received sentence of death, viz Thomas Beck and Peter Robinson for highway robbery, Dorothy Fossett for stealing two guineas from a person in drink; Richard Wentland for a street robbery; Ann his wife for forcibly taking £10; James Philips and William Hurst for stealing goods...Hurst was held at the bar to receive sentence and died on the back of one who was carrying him to the cells. The 2 women pleaded their bellies; Wentland only was found pregnant. 25 ordered for transportation, 3 burnt in the hand and 4 to be whipt.

The only flickers of humanity were seen in the 'pleading the belly' reference and also in the long-standing facility of benefit of clergy. If a prisoner claimed to be pregnant, she was inspected by a panel of matrons to find proof that she was, and her neck would be saved. As already mentioned, for benefit of clergy, a man in the dock facing a murder charge could have a chance of avoiding death by claiming that he was a clergyman and could recite the 'neck verse' (see page 28).

There is also the question of the insane and indeed the so-called 'criminal insane' in the prisons and other places of custody. Throughout the entire history of our penal systems there has always been, and still is, the contentious issue of the high proportion of prisoners within the prisons (rather than in psychiatric hospitals) who have some form of mental illness. Today, organizations such as the Howard League for Penal Reform regularly report on this subject. But until as recently as the 1950s, it was a cause for great concern and disagreement.

In the years before the development of properly run asylums – in fact, not until the end of the nineteenth century in many ways – a person designated insane might or might not end up in the common prison. Individual cases were dealt with differently. But there are milestones on the way to the creation of Broadmoor in 1863. One high-profile case involving the attempted assassination of George III was instrumental in effecting change. On 15 May 1800, James Hadfield, a man who had served with the Duke of York in the European wars, stopped at a shop belonging to a Mr Harman in Greenhill's Rents, Smithfield, and talked about two pistols he had with him. He said that he had bought them for eight shillings, and that he would clean them and sell them for a profit. He then left one of the guns in the shop, saying it might frighten his wife. He must have seemed a definite eccentric to Mr Harman, but he was not the only man who saw Hadfield on this day; in another shop he bought some gunpowder and spoke cryptically about 'a particular business' he had to see to on that day. He drank brandy and went on his way.

The particular business became clear to all present at Drury Lane theatre that night when Hadfield, terribly scarred on the face from his battle experience, stood on a bench, pointed a gun at King George III who had just arrived at the theatre, and fired. George had been responding to the cheers of the crowd, and the bullet missed him by about a foot, lodging in the plaster above him. This happened as the national anthem was being played. Within seconds, courtiers had covered the king and moved into protective positions. Hadfield was grabbed by several people, including two musicians, and dragged away to the music room after being hurled over the rails of the orchestra pit.

James Hadfield saw the Duke of York, the king's son, approach, and said, 'God bless your royal highness, I like you very well, you are a good fellow. This is not the worst that is brewing.' As witnesses spoke at the trial in the hands of Lord Kenyon, it became increasingly clear that Hadfield was deranged. He had received his worst wounds in a fight near Lisle and had been so severely injured that he had been left for dead. It was known in some quarters that he had suffered mental problems since that day. In court, it appeared to the prosecution that he knew exactly what he was doing and had planned an assassination: after all, he had spoken to people en route to the theatre, and he had chosen the best spot in the place from which to fire at the royal box.

The charge was treason, because the man had 'imagined the death of the king' as the Treason Act stated. But Hadfield claimed that he had not planned to kill King George. There had to be testimony from two witnesses that he had planned and attempted the murder, because the offence was treason; but that also enabled him to have two lawyers defend him, and he was fortunate in having Thomas Erskine lead the defence. He was a very talented lawyer, the son of the Earl of Buchan; he had served in the navy, but he changed careers to study law and was admitted to Lincoln's Inn in 1775. He was called to the bar in 1778 and he made his reputation with his defence of Thomas Baillie who had published an attack on Lord Sandwich with regard to abuses in the government of the Greenwich hospital.

But Erskine would have his work cut out with the Hadfield case. Luckily, some of the testimony, such as that by a Mr Wright, made it clear that Hadfield had been 'very confused and agitated' while standing on the bench in the theatre. People nearby had assumed he was there because he wanted the best view of the king, but the facts seemed to be otherwise. However, it was Hadfield's behaviour in court that began to turn things in his favour. He had sat and stared into space, seemingly unconcerned that he was potentially about to be sentenced to be hanged, drawn and quartered. But it was the testimony of the Duke of York that turned the matter towards the issue of insanity. The duke reported what had been said in the music room when the man had been restrained. He said that Hadfield had said he was 'tired of life' and that he 'only regretted the fate of the woman who would shortly be his wife'. What begins to emerge is a picture of a tough soldier who had, in the vocabulary of the twenty-first century, suffered 'post traumatic stress disorder', and other statements made it clear that all was not well in the accused's mind. For instance, Joseph Richardson said that Hadfield had said of the Duke of York, 'God bless him he is the soldier's friend and love!' and had said he had no desire to kill the king.

There had been a frenzy of shooting, though. Other bullets were found, one being in the box occupied by Lady Milner. At that point it must have seemed that, although Hadfield had done and said some very strange things, insanity was not really evident, and there had been rational planning of the act.

But then Erskine spoke. He focused on the question of intention:

did Hadfield have a malicious intent to murder the king or was he governed by a 'miserable and melancholy insanity'? Erskine had the full biography of this tragically crazed ex-soldier; he said that Hadfield's real intention had been suicide on that night at the theatre, and that he had conceived the idea that if he fired near the king, he would be arrested and killed, so the suicide would be done in that way. He had thought of firing over the king's coach, for instance.

But then came the material on the personal life of the accused. Apparently, Erskine said, the man had tried to kill his own daughter just a few days before this attempted killing, and this was done because he thought 'his time had come and he did not want to leave the child behind'. Erskine had a long line of friends and military colleagues who then came to speak, and a full picture emerged of a mind unhinged. One soldier testifying said he had heard Hadfield say that he was King George, calling for a looking glass, and feeling for a crown on his head. Another man said that he had seen the accused 'in a paroxysm of madness' trying to kill him with a bayonet. Other army witnesses stated that Hadfield had been an ideal and excellent soldier before the fight at Lisle. This was all said of a man who had once been a royal orderly to the duke – now a sad discharged soldier with horrible disfigurements and a profoundly disturbed state of mind.

The notion of insanity was therefore before the court. The succession of witness statements on that theme had persuaded Lord Kenyon that this was a man who was mentally insane, and he said that Hadfield could not be found guilty. His destiny was not a date with the axe or the rope, but a journey to Newgate and then Bedlam, from where he would never emerge again into normal life.

The result of the Hadfield case was that, only four days after the trial, a Bill was passed with a long title: 'A bill for regulating trials for High Treason and Misprision of High Treason in certain cases, and for the safe custody of Insane Persons charged with Offences'. The main part of this became the Criminal Lunatics Act of 1800. This established the idea of the lunatic being kept at His Majesty's Pleasure, and although it anticipated in some ways the McNaghten Rules (1843), which established a definition of insanity, it was not accurate or learned on the matter of what constituted insanity. But it did require the detention of an insane person, the disposition being done without any work on the part of the judge: it was an automatic destination for men like Hadfield. Before this Act, any person acquitted because of insanity simply walked free unless the judge wanted the person detained: in that case there had to be a civil hearing. The only option open to the court was to use the 1744 Vagrancy Act, which enabled criminals to be detained in a house of correction. But as a defence, a claim of insanity was very difficult to establish. It was a matter of the expertise of the lawyer and, even then, proving insanity before a felony such as murder or treason was very hard. Luckily for Hadfield, he had plenty of people to speak for him, and it was only because the charge was treason, not murder, that there was full opportunity for a sound defence to be arranged. He had arguably the best legal mind in the land on his side too. Lord Birkenhead, writing in 1910, pointed out the significance of the case: 'This brief, real-life tragedy is unique…it brought a royal Duke into the witness-box and a former royal orderly into the dock.'

Before the notions of 'His Majesty's Pleasure' and criminal lunatics, the annals of the insane in court and in prison make painful reading. For centuries the courts, without any real medical knowledge as advice, nor any understanding of insanity and its treatment, filled the prisons with the mentally ill as well as with real criminals. But to take a positive spin on this, it has to be said that those found insane were sent to bridewells rather than to the gallows or to the transportation ships. Asylums were used as well, of course, as is shown in the case of Susanah Millicent, who stole a petticoat in 1794; she was deranged when finally fit to stand in court, but the lawyers and jury saw that she should be acquitted and confined as insane.

3

Enemies of the State

After the fall of the Bastille and the first stages of the French Revolution in 1789, the next thirty years brought a series of repressive laws in Britain as paranoia, fear of a knock-on-effect revolution and widespread treason grew. In the 1790s there were proclamations against seditious literature, and habeas corpus was suspended (meaning that people could be tried *in absentia*); in 1795 the notion of treason was extended to cover spoken and written words and the two Combination Acts of 1799 and 1800 prevented gatherings in public of groups of more than six people.

The criminal law followed suit; since the mid-eighteenth century there had been a proliferation of capital crimes, but in the Regency years there were yet more statutes. There were also dozens of Acts to prevent 'seditious assemblies' and this led to arrests, assaults and a swelling of the prison population. At the most notorious of these gatherings was Peterloo, a meeting at St Peter's Fields in Manchester in 1819 which was intended as a peaceful meeting, but the crowd numbered some 60,000 and the authorities reacted by sending in the local yeomanry to arrest the main speaker, Henry Hunt, and then anarchy was feared so the hussars went to help, swords drawn. The result was that eleven people were killed and over four hundred injured.

One result of all this was that the prisons had a growing number of radical intellectuals in their cells. In addition to this, these revolutionary enemies of the state, as they were perceived, were complemented by another massive influx of prisoners: soldiers and sailors of Napoleon's army and, in 1812, American prisoners also, because in that year we were at war with the United States as well.

As far as local prisons were concerned, Sir Robert Peel's Gaol Act of 1823 at last put down rules for the management of these places, with inmates classified and separated according to sex, age and the nature of offences. But the government had to cater for the prisoners of war, so specific prisons were used, along with old decommissioned ships, known as 'hulks'.

This new category of prisoner was labelled either military or political, but the latter group only by the radicals themselves. In other words, such prisoners as Chartists (in the 1830s) or writers often considered themselves to be 'political' and therefore to be exempt from prison labour. One of the most important events in this period was the trouble caused by the Chartist prisoners, notably by William Martin. What has become known as the Sheffield Plot of 1840 involved Samuel Holberry, William Martin, Thomas Booker and others devising an attempted coup in Sheffield in which they planned to seize the town hall and the Fortune Inn, set fire to the magistrates court, and then, linking with other Chartists, form an insurrection also in Nottingham and Rotherham. Their plot was betrayed by James Allen, and Lord Howard, the Lord Lieutenant, took immediate action. The result was that, at York assizes on 22 March 1840, Holberry was sentenced to four years at Northallerton for seditious conspiracy: 'and at the expiration of that period to be bound himself in £50 and to find two sureties in ten shillings each, to keep the peace towards his Majesty's subjects'. He was leniently treated; under an Act of 1351, he could have had life imprisonment.

The Chartists wanted electoral reform and mainly worked for votes for working men, along with the reform or electoral districts. In the years around 1840, the 'Physical Force' arm of that movement was accelerating and the Sheffield men were out to take extreme measures. William Martin was given a sentence of one year at Northallerton and he became such a problem that the issue reached

Parliament. His charge was seditious language and his behaviour in court tells us a great deal about the man. *The Times* reported:

> On sentence being passed, he struck his hand on the front of the dock, saying, 'Well that will produce a revolution, if anything will.' He begged his Lordship not to send him to Northallerton, but to let him remain in the castle at York, saying that he was very comfortable, and having been seven months confined already was quite at home.

That was a certain way to open up the Northallerton sojourn, as the judges came down hard on Chartists and they would have had no consideration for these radicals' comfort. Martin went to Northallerton, and there stirred things up. In court he had already stressed his Irish connections and made reference to Irish issues: he entered into 'a long harangue' on Orangemen, the King of Hanover and Rathcormac.

Martin refused to work on the treadwheel as he had not been sentenced to hard labour and thus such a punishment did not fall into that category (see page 89). He was put into the refractory cell for that refusal, but his case was supported by the Secretary of State, Lord Normanby, who wrote that '…the prisoner, who was not sentenced to hard labour, cannot legally be placed upon the wheel against his consent…and that if he should refuse to labour upon the wheel, it would be illegal for the prisoner to place him in solitary confinement'. But a visiting magistrate argued against this by quoting one of Peel's recent Prison Acts that allowed for the work done on a treadwheel to be defined as either hard labour or as 'employment for those who are required by law to work for their maintenance…'

Martin, as far as we know, was ultimately compelled to work on the treadwheel, and he claimed savage treatment at the hands of the Northallerton staff:

> One morning as soon as I had left my cell, the Governor's son…took me by the collar and dragged me from the place where I stood and threw me with violence against the wall, and on the following day he told me I must expect different treatment from what I received in York

and he added that men had been reduced to mere skeletons when their term of imprisonment expired and that it should be the case with me…

These local problems in the treatment of prisoners who had committed 'political' crimes such as sedition, libel or even breaches of the Combination Acts, or been involved in illegal trade unions, were the same everywhere; Beverley house of correction had exactly the same issues with their Chartist, Peddie, from Bradford. But leaving politics aside, the fact was that many of these agitators were involved in firearms and some had every intention of pointing their guns at police constables: some even pulled the triggers.

This imprisonment and treatment of radical leaders came to national attention with the case of Henry Hunt, the man who had spoken at the Peterloo Massacre. The focus of attention was Ilchester prison, where Hunt was sent after sentencing. Hunt, known as 'Orator' after his rousing speeches given in London in 1816–17, was born in Wiltshire, and became a radical thinker, believing in what he termed 'mass pressure' – a non-violent concept simply involving a radical line of thought in the minds of the majority: the workers, who had no vote and who were subject to the vagaries of economics and to the severity of the law. He became MP for Blackburn, and while he was in prison writing his memoirs, that town compiled a petition: 500 people complained of the harsh treatment Hunt was subject to in Ilchester. Hunt himself petitioned Parliament as well, such was his miserable state. But he was also revolted by the treatment of other prisoners at the prison. In March 1822, in Parliament, John Hobhouse told the House about the prison:

He called upon the House to look at the total absence of control in the prison. The prisoner was not checked by the surgeon, the surgeon by the coroner, nor the coroner by the magistrates. Let them remember the abuses and cruelties proved: Hillier loaded with irons and beheld, so loaded, without interference from the magistrates, and Mary Cuer, with her new-born child, exposed to cold and hunger. Let members advert to the badness of the bread, and the impurity of the water – to the absence of air and sunshine, and to the presence of

instruments of torture unparalleled but by those brought over in the
Spanish Armada...

There had been an enquiry, and the interviews with staff had highlighted these abuses. William Bridle, the turnkey, was tried for his
cruelties. An old man called Charles Hill, for instance, had been
confined there for fifteen years. He reported that prisoners were
locked up from 5 p.m. to 7 a.m. The prison was built near a river and
parts of it were below water level; the prison was flooded to a depth
of 14 inches, and prison fever often raged there. Sometimes, prisoners
due to appear in court were not taken there for fear of their fever
infecting the assembly at the court.

Mr Alderman Wood told the House, responding to a petition by
another prisoner, that:

> As to the prisoner's own house, there were proofs to show that it was
> kept open to unseasonable hours, and sometimes all night, while it
> was a scene of riot, drunkenness and gambling...it was customary for
> people to gather there to gamble...a clergyman of the neighbourhood
> had lost 18 guineas there one night...

One of the worst atrocities was the case of a man called Gardner,
who had been put in solitary confinement, into a 'dark dungeon',
and then chained to his bed, his head shaved and a 'blister' applied
to his scalp by the hand of another prisoner. This must have been a
plaster of some kind. The man tried to rub it off by scraping his head
on the wall. That made the turnkey apply a straitjacket to the unfortunate man.

These abuses were caused by the new staff – those succeeding a
number of earlier gaolers who appear to have run the prison fairly
well. In 1799, Jane Austen's aunt, Mrs Leigh-Perrot, was detained
there for the alleged theft of twenty shillings' worth of lace from a
shop in Bath. That was serious: she could have been transported or
even hanged for such a crime. Yet she stayed not in a cell but in the
warden's house. But she was refused bail and had to remain in prison
for seven months until her trial; she was acquitted at Taunton assizes

and sent a large sum of money to the gaoler's family. Ilchester was not a den of iniquity in 1807 when Dr Lettsom inspected the place for *The Gentleman's Magazine*. He reported that the rooms were furnished with a bedstead and straw, and that the inmates were washed and the men shaved regularly in the cold or warm baths near the main gate.

By 1819 when Hunt was there, things had changed, and William Bridle was the man responsible. At Wells assizes in August 1822, he appeared in court, charged with 'intent to injure' Mary Cuer and James Hillier. The prosecution was brought for the Crown by the Attorney General. In the case of Hillier, the prisoner had applied the blister – a hot poultice probably – after shutting Hillier in the dark cell, and later fitting a straitjacket. He had shut Mary Cuer, with her new baby, in the dark cell from 10 to 23 November, providing only bread and water. When she was given water, she had to drink it from a bucket. Not surprisingly, with such deprivations in the winter, both mother and child became seriously ill and were lucky to survive.

The magistrates were cleared of any failings and, surprisingly, although Bridle had been sacked in July 1821, they said good things about him. Sir John Acland stated that Bridle was 'an honest and meritorious officer'. Yet strangely, a certain Elizabeth Smith who was to testify in support of Mary did not turn up at court. The jury found Bridle guilty only in the case of Hillier, and a sentence was passed a week later: Bridle was fined £50 and he was to be kept at the Marshalsea until he could pay the sum.

Henry Hunt was released in 1823 and had a party in London. He later published an account of the prison in his book entitled *A Peep into a Prison, or the Inside of Ilchester Bastille*. He was certainly not the only radical to see the inside of a prison. Samuel Bamford, the Lancastrian writer and political activist, saw the inside of several prisons around this time. He found himself in Lincoln Castle at the same time that Hunt was bound for Ilchester, and only a few years before there had been a case of abuse there, in which a Mr Thomas Houlden had been kept in the condemned cell, although he was only there for debt. In that particular case, a magistrate had been responsible, along with the governor. Bamford's worst experience was watching a man hang. He could see Cobb Hall, the tower at a corner of the castle where hangings took place, and in March 1821 he saw the gallows waiting for two men.

Mr Justice Richardson had led the trial of these two men, who had burgled the house of an old woman in Whaplode. Parish, who had been a shepherd working for the victim, wrote to the men he had met in Lancashire, and Bamford explains why that connection was there: 'It was a custom...for harvest men to go from Lancashire to Lincolnshire – a "cwokin" as they called it – and a party of these from Astley Bridge had been in the habit of doing the harvest work...' Bamford notes that the robbers went to the farm dressed as mummers, and then, 'The robbers next tied the inmates fast and plundered the house of about nine hundred pounds worth of plate, money and notes...'

Although they had been masked, one man's mask had fallen off and the man was seen: that was a man called Booth, and he was soon tracked down. Bamford wrote, 'The hounds of the law soon laid on the true scent and set off for Lancashire with the speed but not the noise of bloodhounds.' Some Lancashire men had fled across the sea, but in the end Parish, the shepherd, and Booth found themselves in court and were sentenced to hang.

The events leading to their deaths were seen by Bamford, who described the scene:

> It was rather a cloudy and gusty morning when, getting up to my window, I beheld the gallows fixed, and two halters ready noosed, swinging in the wind. To me, this first sight of the instrument of death was both melancholy and awful...I placed myself on the rampart leading to the tower, on which stood the gallows, and had a full view of the criminals as they crossed the green. First came the Governor, bearing a white wand; then some halberdiers and other sheriff's men, then the deputy sheriff, next came the criminal, then the chaplain, the turnkey, the executioner and assistant...and other javelin men...

Bamford also saw the two felons die: 'The shepherd appeared to have his eyes fixed on the instrument of death from the moment he came in view of it' and 'He appeared faint and required assistance to mount the ascent'. Booth, wearing a blue coat, was 'more dogged in his manner' and 'He held his head a little on one side, gave a glance at the gallows, spat out some white froth…and went on again without help.'

The bodies were removed 'on the backs of men' after they had been left hanging there for an hour. They were laid side by side on the floor of the Town Hall.

The other enemies of Britain were the prisoners of war. During the war with Napoleon, 100,000 French prisoners were held captive in Britain. For many officers, there was a parole arrangement, and although the French did not reciprocate, the British authorities maintained it. There was formerly a prisoner exchange system, but that stopped in 1803 and so prison space had to be found for these vast numbers of men. After the Battle of Trafalgar in 1805, some five thousand men were transferred to Britain.

The responsibility for accommodating the prisoners was given to the Transport Board, an organization working closely with the Admiralty. There were some war prisons, at Millbay, Stapleton, Forton and Portchester, but in 1797 a huge prison camp was created at Norman Cross near Peterborough, and then others were built: Dartmoor, Valleyfield and Perth. By 1814 there were nine such prisons, and Dartmoor, arguably the most notorious, had almost eight thousand prisoners of war by 1814.

More space was needed, however, and so the hulks were used. Of the various types of ships, the three-deckers were the largest, and they held 1,200 men. Incredibly, by 1814 there were fifty-one hulks in use. A massive problem of ill health arose, perhaps more outstandingly so compared with harsh conditions and punishments in general. The Enlightenment thinking, with its humanitarian basis, was not always a matter of theory turning into applied reformed actions, but in this case a lawyer called Emerich de Vattel had published *Le Droit des Gens* (The Rights of People) in 1758 and this was influential. Linked to this there had been the exchange system, which meant that there would simply be a short time of internment, and there had been the *parole d'honneur* – officers being released on their word of honour that they would not re-enlist and fight in the current conflict.

The Transport Board had to cope with the frustrating paradox that French prisoners could be released by parole, by exchanges or as invalids, but the French did not act in the same way. By 1803, 500 French officers had been released on *parole d'honneur*. But the fact remains that traditional prisoner-of-war procedure broke down. History is always biased and partisan, and the French writing on the lives of French prisoners in Britain insist on the treatment being brutal and heartless. But at times this contradicts the British records. For instance, one French writer wrote about prisoners on HMS *Prothee*: 'These…dead people come out for a moment from their graves, hollow-eyed, earthy complexioned, round-backed, unshaven, their frames barely covered with yellow rags, their bodies frightfully thin.'

Worst of all, allegedly, was the terrifying Dartmoor prison. Reports and letters to the press constantly argued that the regime there was barbarous. One opinion was, 'Men fit for service are killed, and then sent home to France to finish dying there.' But there were other prisons with bad reputations. General Pillet wrote that Norman Cross, for instance, was a place where he had seen 4,000 French prisoners buried. In 2010, the television archaeology programme *Time Team* set out to test the truth of this by conducting a 'dig' there. The prison at Norman Cross was constructed between 1796 and 1797 to accommodate 7,000 prisoners; it was known at the time as Yaxley barracks, only 78 miles north of London and close to the sea, so communications and supply were not difficult. Great Yarmouth was to become a receiving port for prisoners, and they were taken to Lynn by sea and then by canal to Peterborough. But some had to walk, as this record shows: 'At Lynn the prisoners were packed into barges and lighters and were sent up river through the Forty Foot and the Paupers' Cut and the Nene to Peterborough, whence they marched to Norman Cross.'

The French were allowed victualling each day to the value of seven pence and the total cost per man per day was one shilling and ten pence. They lived on bread, biscuits and some beef, but it is recorded that much of this was inedible. George Borrow, the Norfolk writer, noted that, 'The men's rations was of carrion meat and bread from which I have seen the very hounds turn away.' The local newspaper, *The Stamford Mercury*, gives us an insight into the place as over three thousand prisoners arrived in 1797: 'Exclusive of seven dead and three who escaped they passed under the care of seven turnkeys and the 80 men of the Caithness legion who guarded the Norman Cross.' These guards were 'fencibles' (regiments raised under the threat of invasion) who had served in Ireland, and were under the command of Sir Benjamin Dunbar.

For such large numbers of prisoners, more military presence was needed; the Dragoon Guards and Oxford Militia were also present, the latter men escorting prisoners from Yarmouth. Later, Dutch prisoners were also brought to Norman Cross. The numbers were certainly high, but what of the belief that there was a burial ground there for 4,000 dead, as claimed by the French? The researchers from the *Time Team* venture found no hard evidence at all, but the possibility has still not been ruled out.

The Transport Board also had to cope with corruption: the problems lay not with the prison staff themselves, but with the contractors. The stipulated dietary in reality rarely met the demands of the orders placed, so that often meat orders would be replaced by herring or cod, or even by vegetables. The Board did try hard to regulate matters, having regular inspections, often visiting prisons unannounced – as happens today. The Board had a doctor in their ranks, Dr John Weir, and he also investigated and reported on prisons. He sacked surgeons who were clearly incompetent, such as Jeffcott at Stapleton and Kirkwood on the *Europa* hulk at Portsmouth.

There is no doubt that in the hulks there was a terrible death toll. In the Portsmouth hulks between 1817 and 1827 there were 222 deaths and 188 of these were due to illness. Of these, 115 died from one of these killers: pneumonia, consumption, dysentery and typhus. The inquest records, held at the Sign of the Packet Boat inn, show the extent of the illnesses and deaths. The mortality rates in all the prisons were high, but Dartmoor was the worst in that respect.

Sir Thomas Tyrwhitt, Lord Warden of the Stanneries, thought that a farming community could be made on Dartmoor, with Princetown at the centre, but that did not work out, and so when the notion of a convict prison was broached, costs were done, and it transpired that running a prison was much cheaper than maintaining several convict ships. So work went ahead, and builders were still there when the first French prisoners arrived in 1808. The result was a powerful fortress, with barracks for the militia. The prison had two high circular walls, five blocks, a hospital and staff quarters. There was no heating in the cells, and things got off to a bad start as 1,500 men were packed into cells meant for just 1,000.

In the hospital there was work for several nurses and washermen, and the latter were paid six pence a day, but their bonus was that they could share the clothing of the dead. Next to the hospital was a place feared by all. This was known as the 'cachot' – a sort of 'black hole' of massive stone blocks with a metal door, and this punishment cell was for the escapees who were caught, and for serious breaches of discipline such as assaults on warders.

The governor was in the service of the Transport Office, but was also a captain in the navy. From the very beginning, as the motto over the gate says – 'spare the vanquished' – the ideology behind it was as much ruled by caring as by punishment. But things easily went wrong, as they do in all prisons. There were frequent deaths, many due to smallpox, but the total of fatalities between 1808 and 1815 was the staggering number of 1,500. As Trevor James, historian of the prison, has said, 'More than fifty years later their bones littered the area, having been exposed by Dartmoor weather and wild animals.'

The rations at Dartmoor were 'navy rations' – mostly soup, fish and bread – but there were wages for work, so prisoners could buy and sell food at certain times as well. The daily ration was a pound of bread, two pounds of fish, a pound of potatoes and vegetables. Unlike civilian prisons, though, the discipline was organized by the prisoners themselves; rules were established and infringements were punished by flogging with hammock cords. Conditions and supplies were affected by corruption of course, and one of the worst cases was that of a contractor called Josh Rowe, whose malpractice was reported by the governor, Captain Cotgrave. As a rule, the Transport Office did an admirable job of dealing with contractors. Their advertisements for tenders stressed that, 'Each tender must be accompanied by a letter from two respectable persons, engaging to become bound with the person tendering, in the sum of £2,000 for the due performance of the contract.' Josh Rowe continued to exploit the system and Cotgrave had endless problems with him. After all, the dietary is a crucially important part of a prison regime: adequate food is essential to well-being and reduces the chance of trouble and rebellion.

To illustrate the effects of adulterated food on the morale of prisoners, the tale one former inmate told shows how bad things could be: 'One day a man pulled out of the soup bucket of his mess a dead rat which he held up by the tail, whereupon heads and tails and feet were dredged up from every bucket…'

In Dartmoor's history as a place for prisoners of war, though, the story that darkens the whole story, with horrendous and barbaric repression, is the occasion in April 1815 when American sailors – who had been drafted into service with the British navy but who resented that and preferred to be prisoners of war – were taken to Dartmoor. There, they repeatedly made attempts to escape. Americans were taken to Dartmoor from 1813 until 1815. Britain had had the task of deciding what should be done with American prisoners from the beginning; at Dartmoor the Americans were segregated, with the blacks being placed in barrack number 4. The long room would have had a central area slung with hammocks, and there was a lot of illness as the temperature was very high at times. The blacks had been brought in by privateers, and they were at first mixed across the prison population but, when segregated, communication was of course easier and concerted action and revolt could be planned.

Such was the status of blacks at the time that at Dartmoor the blacks' barrack was used for punishment: in April 1815 the records show that three Frenchmen had been found in the act of buggery and were flogged, and when put with the 'blacks' 'turned in amongst the negroes'. But as the prisoners controlled punishment most of the time, they were responsible for some of the most severe sentences within the walls, as in the case of one man who stole ten pounds. He was to be flogged with 500 lashes, but the punishment was cut down after the first 75, so there could be some healing before the next lashing.

Barrack 4 became a strong community, at one time led by a man called King Dick. He was very tall and strong, and the records show that he had 'two comely lads' with him as an escort.

By March 1815 there was a plan to return the American prisoners but, before that could happen, the horrible events of April took place. Captain Thomas Shortland suffered the complaints of prisoners that the bread issue was poor. There was a feeling of unease about the place, and when a hole was found in a wall, one leading to another yard rather than the open moor, Shortland treated it as an escape attempt, and as some of the black Americans were by the gates of their yard, he ordered troops to open fire. Seven prisoners died and thirty-one were wounded. One of the prisoners who died was only fourteen years old. The irony was that just three months earlier, the peace treaty between Britain and the United States had been signed.

There is no argument that can possibly condone what the officer did that day, but it is certain that escapes of prisoners was a frequent occurrence and there was plenty of local confrontation between French paroled officers and British civilians, but none of that applied to American prisoners, so it is unlikely that there was a grudge darkening the heart of Shortland.

The years between the French Revolution and the Battle of Waterloo, then, saw a massive influx of prisoners into the prisons and hulks who were not the average type of crook, or destitute and desperate waifs; they were not even debtors. These prisoners were either soldiers or sailors, or intellectuals who wanted social and political change. The repression was savage and ruthless. What shows this more than anything else is the fate of some of the Luddites at York. In 1812, the clothing industry of the West Riding faced the implications of the arrival of new machinery in the finishing processes of clothing manufacture: many of them did so with a resolve to fight the mechanization. What some of them did in that zeal to survive was bring a reign of terror to villages and mills from the Pennines to the Halifax and Bradford areas. In order to defeat them, the forces of law had to bring in the militia, such was the fear across the county. The year 1812 was a time of particularly strained and repressive economic measures and poorer families were suffering. It might seem strange to mention that many of the Luddites were quite well off, but they feared the future and they did not stand idly by while the greater macroeconomic factors crushed them.

They took their name from a fabled character called Ned Ludd who reputedly led similar machine-wrecking attacks in Nottingham. But, arguably, a leader came on the scene in the Spen Valley who was to conduct a campaign of profound fear-instilling aggression against those employers who had new machinery installed. The focus for the campaign was the trade linked to the cloth finishing processes, in particular the shearers, of whom Mellor was one. This was a skilled business, demanding the expert use of large and unwieldy shears for trimming and finishing.

Mellor realized that the essence of success in these attacks was secrecy, because the communities along the valleys where the clothing industry flourished would all know each other well from communal occasions. He therefore had his men black their faces and always wear hats; they would then attack by night. The reign of terror lasted for some time and the local magistrates were at a loss as to what to do, but the chain of command broadened and the reaction of the authorities spread from the West Riding to the militia, and then to the Lord Lieutenant of the county at Wentworth Woodhouse, and eventually to the Home Secretary.

After various delays that gave the Luddites the upper hand, sheer paranoia eventually led to positive action; first it was due to military successes as a brutal and repressive group of militia conducted their own reprisals, and then, with the new Home Secretary Lord Sidmouth at the Home Office, the establishment began to create an equal measure of fear in the Luddites. Soon it was a case of the magistrates finding men willing to give information, and Lord Sidmouth was keen on the use of spies functioning as *agents provocateurs*.

Matters were made worse as deaths occurred: notably, there had been a murder of a factory owner called Horsfall, and Mellor, along with William Thorpe and Thomas Smith, was charged. Horsfall had been attacked on the road, shot by men positioned alongside in undergrowth. Witnesses came forward to implicate Mellor, a man who had also been pointed at by a particular turncoat and petty thief from the village of Flockton. These three men were convicted of murder and found guilty. One commentator writing in the 1830s wrote: 'It is impossible to read the details of this and the other Luddite cases without shuddering at the cold-hearted and systematic manner in which the murders were debated and agreed on...'

Mellor, Smith and Thorpe were hanged on 8 January 1813. They were led to the scaffold still in their irons, and they all went down on their knees after the chaplain asked them to pray. Mellor said, 'Some of my enemies may be here. If they be, I freely forgive them, and all the world, and I hope the world will forgive me.' The bodies were taken to York County Hospital for dissection.

On 16 January of that same year, fourteen men were hanged on the conviction of taking illegal oaths and the destruction of a mill; in addition, there was a charge of riot, of course. Eight men were found guilty of riot and destruction at Cartwright's Mill, with the story featuring in Charlotte Bronte's novel entitled *Shirley*. There were attempts to provide alibis when several defence witnesses were called, but all that failed, and it took the jury just five minutes to decide on a guilty verdict. As was noted by several historians in earlier times, all the men were married and all left young children fatherless. The word 'Luddite' entered the language, such was the impact of that year of terror when the middle classes in the valleys of the West Riding could not sleep easily in their beds.

Such was the suppression conducted by the paranoid and fearful government of Britain that many feared open rebellion in the streets. Thousands of prisoners of war were held in hulks and barracks, and thousands more unfortunates who openly demanded a fairer and more equal society languished in prisons across the land.

In more recent times, trials of traitors have been more complex. Perhaps one of the most difficult, in terms of the interpretation of the law, was that of Sir Roger Casement during the First World War: here was a man who was 'hanged by a comma' and whose time in prison made him a dark version of celebrity.

After the Easter Rising in Dublin in 1916, the British government were savage in their reprisals. The war with Germany was of course demanding their full attention – and, paradoxically, thousands of Irish men had signed up and were fighting in the trenches for Britain and her Empire – when their countrymen took up arms in order to create a free Republican Ireland. After some hard fighting in the streets of Dublin, thousands were imprisoned, and in May the executions began. On 3 May, Patrick Pearse, Thomas MacDonagh and Thomas Clarke were shot in the yard at Kilmainham jail, in Dublin. Other perceived leaders were shot over the next few days and then, on 6 May, no other executions were announced. Eighteen men who were scheduled to die found that their sentences were commuted, two of these being for life.

There was pressure from America. England needed her American allies to help fight the war in Europe, and Irish America did not like the executions at all. But the shootings did go on, the most disgusting being the death of James Connolly, brought out from his sick bed into the Kilmainham yard to be shot; he had been driven across the city in an ambulance, then sat on a chair in the yard, shot even though he was unable to stand. Courts-martial and death sentences continued. But a level of leniency then came in, and even Eamon de Valera was saved; he had been a primary leader in the Rising, in command at Boland's Mill.

In total there were more than three thousand arrests in 1916, but many were released, and over fifteen hundred were interned in England. One person, though, stood out as an extraordinary case: Sir Roger Casement. He had been engaging in liaisons with Germany, and the Rising had, as part of its statements of identity and aspirations, made Germany appear to be their ally. Casement was arrested for high treason and his trial took place on 29 June, the prosecution being led by F. E. Smith (later Lord Birkenhead). Casement's situation was bizarre and contradictory: he had received a knighthood from King George V, but insisted that his only country, his own real allegiance, was Ireland.

He had enjoyed an unbelievably interesting and adventurous life prior to his involvement with the 1916 Rising; in 1914 he had tried to create a Liberal party in Ulster, as well as his adventures farther afield. But in his trial he claimed that his ultimate aim was to serve Ireland. He had tried to recruit an Irish Brigade in Germany, and he failed in that. In visiting the POW camps in Germany, he had been unwelcome and, as was noted at the time, he had to have a guard with him on those visits in his attempts to divert the prisoners of war from their duty.

Casement had gone to Germany, his movements monitored by British spies, and when he returned to Ireland it had been in a U-boat, landing off the coast of Kerry, where he was soon arrested. His earlier life and career had been extraordinary; he had made the world aware of atrocities in the Congo and in South America, and he was something of a hero, particularly in America. He had made friends and contacts in high places. It seemed outrageous and incredible that such a man should be a traitor.

The basis of his indictment was the Treason Act of 1351 which states that the offence is defined by 'compassing or imagining the King's death' and 'levying war against the King in the realm' but also, and this was the crucially important clause for Casement, 'adhering to the King's enemies in his realm, giving them aid and comfort, here and elsewhere'. That comma, and what followed, was his death sentence. 'Elsewhere' was easily defined in a way that included activities at sea, in Germany and in fact in Ireland, so loose was the definition of the word.

His trial has been the subject of a vast literature, including an account by F. E. Smith himself, published soon after the events, along with other famous trials in history. Smith recalled the issue of whether or not Casement had actually committed treason, and he expressed the situation in this way:

> When I closed the case for the prosecution, the legal argument began. It was necessarily long, technical and intricate. It involved the true leaning of the Treason Act, which was originally drawn up in Norman French. It necessitated a minute examination of a number of musty statutes, long since repealed…It was essential to grasp the details of an antiquated procedure…

Eventually, agreement was reached; the dates of earlier precedents in treason trials had to be noted, and ultimately the wording that was used against Casement was 'adhering to the King's enemies'. When the sentence finally came, it was done after much deliberation, as Smith wrote: '...after Counsel's speeches and a judicial summing up by Lord Reading in terms most scrupulously fair and impartial, the jury convicted and Casement was sentenced to death'.

Casement went to Pentonville. An appeal was launched, presided over by the famous Lord Darling. The question was still there: had Casement's actions been an infringement of the law? He had been known to the public as a 'servant of the Crown', as Dudley Barker wrote. But the fact was that on 20 April 1916, near Tralee Bay, a labourer looking out to sea had seen a flashing light, and a farmer walking home later saw a boat a few yards from the shore. He beached the boat and there he found three Mauser pistols, maps of Ireland, a flash lamp and a flag. There was a jacket, and in one pocket there was a railway ticket from Berlin to Wilhelmshaven. At a time of spy mania on the Home Front of the Great War, that story was enough to condemn Casement as being the owner of those materials, and as the person who had landed. He tried to claim, when the police cornered him, that he was a writer, on holiday, from his home in Buckinghamshire.

It had all been a daring and bold adventure, but now he was in court, fighting for his life. Darling soon dismissed the arguments of the appeal lawyers for Casement, saying:

I am unaware of anything in the history of the German nation during this war which would lead me to accept with enthusiasm the suggestion that they would be prepared to offer unlimited hospitality to a number of Irish soldiers in order that when the war was over they would be able to write a new page in the purely domestic history of their country.

Casement was asked if he had anything to say before a decision was reached and a sentence passed. He had had three weeks in prison in which to prepare a speech. His defence counsel, Sullivan, had tried to argue that no matter what a man did, at the time the 1851 statute was passed, he was out of the king's realm and so could not be tried for treason. Darling and the other judges disagreed.

Casement went back to Pentonville, and just a short time before he was hanged he was accepted into the Roman Catholic Church. In his time in the prison, two of Casement's cousins wrote to the prison to ask permission to visit him and to send some clothes. The requests met with no answer, but Gavan Duffy kept fighting to have these requests accepted and considered, and finally Casement was allowed a visit. But when they did arrive, he still had on the clothes he wore when he was arrested. They had sent clothes, but he had not had them. It took another complaint for the clothes to be found, and then for him to put them on.

The man with the task of hanging Casement was the Rochdale hangman, John Ellis, who had executed Dr Crippen. A local man in Rochdale was asked what he thought about the Casement affair and Ellis. He said, 'Jack were very patriotic you know. He said he'd willingly give £10 to charity for the chance to hang Casement. He wer' as pleased as Punch when he got t'job. He went off to London as happy as a schoolboy.' The hangman travelled to Pentonville, and there he went with the governor to watch Casement, pacing in his cell; the purpose of that inspection was to ascertain the right length of drop for the man's height and weight. Ellis decided on a drop of 6 feet 5 inches.

On the last evening of Casement's life, a Father McCarroll stayed with him; the prisoner could not sleep and before 8 a.m. of the appointed day he was in the chapel, and he prayed with the priest until his death at 9 p.m. This was on 3 August. Casement's last words were, 'God save Ireland! Jesus receive my soul...' Ellis reported that Casement went to his death with great courage.

The Times reported on the end:

By 8 o'clock a crowd had begun to assemble in Caledonian Road, which runs in front of the prison...about 150 people, chiefly women and children from the immediate neighbourhood, stood on the footpath and fixed their gaze on the prison walls...Near to where they had stood was a group of workmen, who on hearing the bell raised a cheer. Five minutes afterwards the crowd had disappeared and the street resumed its normal appearance.

The usual official notices were posted outside the prison, confirming that the judgement of death was executed. Then there was an inquest, held in the prison, supervised by Walter Schroder. Gavan Duffy, a friend of Casement, identified the body, and then asked if he could read a statement. This dialogue then followed:

> Coroner: The order for the burial is issued by me and handed to the governor. As to any other matter in reference to the burial of the body, any application must be made to the authorities.
> Duffy: I appreciate that, Sir, I have applied to the Home Office for permission to have his body. I consider it a monstrous act of indecency to refuse it.
> Coroner: On that I cannot express any opinion. There was clearly a great deal of bitterness at the whole affair. Duffy wanted to know whether Casement had been considered to be insane during his time in prison, and Dr Mander, senior medical officer at Pentonville, said that there was no truth in that.

What could have been more banal after that than the simple statement that, at the corner's hearing, a verdict of 'death by execution' was confirmed. A petition for a reprieve had been put together in Ireland, and after Casement's death there was clearly a great deal of ill feeling in his homeland.

4

THE RULE OF SILENCE, SEPARATION AND THE PENITENTIARY

It seems such a simple ruling: no talking. However, if you imagine it in the context of life in prison, then the implications are enormously traumatic. It is perhaps more hard to bear than a corporal punishment. The imposition of silence means that human communication is banned. Anthropologists tells us that 'phatic communication' – the interaction between people that bonds relationships – is crucially important to the well-being of any community. If a prisoner is not allowed to speak, then his or her ability to express emotion, request help, share problems is denied. Silence compels an inner dialogue: it may lead to mental ill health and, in some cases, serious insanity. Even more than this, it prevents catharsis; it cancels any potential unloading of remorse.

In the British prison system, the years of the silent and separate systems often led to exactly that – an astonishing increase in mental illness. The withdrawal of talk is double-edged. In the nineteenth century, when prison was very much influenced by religious principles, silence was a desirable part of self-reflection. Its supposed virtues were explained in Robert Browning's poem, *Abt Vogler*:

> Well, it is earth with me, silence resumes her reign;
> I will be patient and proud, and soberly acquiesce.

Those lines could almost be a definition of what the prison authorities wanted in the mindset of their charges. But the other and far less acceptable edge of the concept is about what happens when speech is taken away. Deprive a person of the outlet of social talk and a self-preoccupied internal monologue develops, an implosion that encourages fantasy in its more harmful expression.

Little of this was known c. 1840. All that mattered to the governors and others in power was that nothing should disturb the prison regime. As many prison officers have said through the ages, 'Happiness is a closed cell door.' Many would add to that, 'Happiness is silence, as hard work goes on.'

Think of a prison and often thoughts immediately turn to the person at the top: the governor. Today the management of a prison is about co-operation between the new breed of governors (often people who have no background in prison work) and the prison officers and their union. In the years before the nationalization of prisons (1877), the governor or keeper was lord of all he surveyed. His word was beyond challenge or dissent. The wretches brought into his institution had already experienced a long spell in prison waiting for the next assizes for what was called 'prison delivery, *oyez and terminer*'. That meant that judges on the road, on the assize circuits across the country, cleared the prisons of the rotting prisoners and sorted out any outstanding cases involving legal process and argument.

The keeper of the house of correction or local prison would have as his charges half-starved and weak villains, poor debtors, riff-raff vagrants inside from their lives of begging, and also a number of recalcitrant rogues who would have to be subdued by various methods of crushing body and soul.

The prison memoirs of the Regency period often contain accounts such as this:

A close, warm air, tainted with an abominable odour, was the first thing that saluted my senses on entering this wretched place. It was a small cell, perhaps four or five yards in length, by two or three in width, and probably as lofty as it was long. Opposite the door was an aperture to let in a stinted quantity of air…in the centre was a stove with a fire in, and in a corner was the convenience from which emanated the disagreeableness first mentioned. Two or three fellows were stretched on the benches, one doubled up in a corner and one lay like a dog…

LINCOLNSHIRE,   LINDSEY TO WIT.
CALENDAR OF PRISONERS

AT KIRTON OCTOBER SESSIONS,
ON FRIDAY THE 17TH DAY OF OCTOBER, 1851.

The letter N. denotes the prisoner cannot read or write.—*Imp,* read, or read or write imperfectly.—*Well,* read or write well.—*Sup,* superior education.—The letter *h. l.* hard labour.—The asterisk the number of times the prisoner has been committed.—The parallel lines those who have been convicted of felony.—

READ AND WRITE.	NAMES.	WHEN COMMITTED	OFFENCES.	COMMITTING MAGISTRATE.	SENTENCES.
Imp	1 James Riley	16 July 7th	Stealing at Gainsborough, one Silver Watch, the property of James Whiley.	Rev. G. Hutton	
N	2 William Andrews	25 July 12th	Stealing at Gainsborough, three pieces of Silver coin called Shillings, two pieces of Copper coins called Pennys, one other piece of Copper coin called a Halfpenny, and one Gown, the property of Elizabeth Wilson.	Rev. C. W. Hudson	
N	3 Mary Ann Andrews	22 July 12th			
Imp	4 John Drury*	23 July 17th	Stealing at Barrow, one Bacon Ham, a quantity of threshed Wheat, and a Calico Bag, the property of John Robinson.	S. Wormald, Esq.	
N	5 James Maw	24 July 22nd	Stealing at Barton, two pieces of Gold coin called Sovereigns, and seven pieces of Silver coin called Shillings, the property of James Maw, senior.	G. C. Uppleby, Esq.	
Imp	6 Elizabeth Thompson	60 July 24th	Uttering at Gainsborough, a certain piece of false & counterfeit coin resembling a Crown piece, and having other pieces of false and counterfeit Coin in her possession, well-knowing them to be false and counterfeit.	H. E. Smith, Esq.	
Imp	7 John Thomas	25 Aug. 1st	Stealing at Haxey, one Brass Pan, the property of Joseph Morris.	Ven. Archden. Stonehouse	
Imp	8 Martha Procea, otherwise Martha Eden	37 Aug. 4th	Stealing at Thonock, twelve yards of Carpet, the property of Henry Bacon Hickman, Esq	H. E. Smith, Esq.	
Imp	9 William Newton	20 Aug. 16th	Stealing at Hibaldstow, one Waistcoat, one Shirt, and other articles, the property of Thomas Hansen.	Sir J. Nelthorpe, Bart.	
Imp	10 Valentine Geddins	25 Sept. 1st	Stealing at Willingham, two Heifers, the property of John Hopkinson.	W. Hutton, Esq.	
Imp	11 William Hill	29 Sept. 1st	Receiving at Willingham, the above Heifers, well-knowing them to have been Stolen, the property of John Hopkinson.	W. Hutton, Esq.	
Imp	12 Thomas Hill *neg?*	60 Sept. 1st			
N	13 Andrew Hart	48 Sept. 9th	Stealing at Thornton, one Jacket, the property of Charles Kirman.	W. D. Field, Esq.	
Imp	14 Elizabeth Cummins	27 Sept. 19th	Stealing at Gainsborough, two pair of Stays, five Blankets, one Woollen Scarf, and other articles, the property of John Moore.	Rev. J. T. Huntley / Rev. J. Stockdale	
Imp	15 John Clay	Sept. 25th	Stealing at Snarford, one Cotton Shirt, the property of Matthew Sharman.	Rev. J. T. Huntley	
Imp	16 James Smith	28 Oct. 9th	Stealing at South Ferriby, one Silk Handkerchief, the property of George Drury.	G. C. Uppleby, Esq.	
N	17 John Uffindele	29 Oct. 13th	Stealing at Ealand, two tame Rabbits, the property of George Crowcroft; also stealing at Crowle, one Turkey, the property of John Branyer; and further charged with stealing at Ealand, one Rabbit, the property of Richard Thornton	G. S. Lister, Esq. / Rev. J. Dobson / T. H. Lister, Esq.	
N	18 Henry Stainforth	30 Oct. 15th	Stealing at Ealand, one tame Rabbit, the property of Richard Thornton; also stealing at Ealand, one tame Rabbit, the property of George Crowcroft.	G. S. Lister, Esq. / Rev. J. Dobson / T. H. Lister, Esq.	
Imp	19 Macarty Daniel	23 Oct. 14th	At Caistor, did attempt feloniously and burglariously to break and enter the Dwelling-house of William Pybus.	Rev. J. T. Hales Tooke	

A calendar of prisoners: from Lincoln assizes. The calendar was a list of prisoners with their offences, place and date of trial, and length of sentences given.

This was a normal lock-up cell, nothing like a solitary one. It was designed to reduce the prisoner to misery of course.

The eighteenth century was a time when sinecures and patronage oiled the wheels of society. Rich men had levees – queues of lesser individuals on the make, lobbying for steady and lucrative positions in the hierarchy of society. The 'Red Book' published and reprinted regularly throughout the Georgian and Regency years listed the occupations that demanded very little and that often allowed the office-holder to spend plenty of time at the races or at the gaming tables rather than actually being at his post.

Prisons were no exception to this, though many jobs were taxing and the conditions were unpleasant. The idea of professional staff, with training, was not yet a concept in the mindset of those who built new prisons, but economy was the first consideration, and nepotism was one way of ensuring that the man in charge controlled costs.

The houses of correction were meant to make money, and the keepers were in total command. Like the new mills of the Industrial Revolution, the places were houses of industry, and were sometimes referred to as that. Often, the prisons were family concerns, and keepers would use their sons, wives, sisters and other relatives to boost the family earnings and, of course, to be sure that they knew their staff, rather than taking a chance by employing a stranger.

Northallerton was first established in 1783, one of the first of the new local prisons in the late Georgian years, and the keeper was George Parkin. By 1805, when a writer from *The Gentleman's Magazine* paid a visit to write a report for his journal, George's son, William, was keeper. At the heart of the prison regime was silence and hard work, and Parkin found a nice little earner for his teenage son, William, destined to be the third Parkin keeper.

Silence was absolutely essential to the system, stemming from the sure belief that a man who kept his thoughts to himself would not cause any trouble and might even start to look into his soul and see the evil dwelling therein. Young William's position was keeper of silence. It was his constant insistence that no one should utter a single syllable, not even if the speaker wanted to start a discussion on something in the Bible.

At the start of his career, William wrote to his friend in York about his work in the prison. He gave a vivid account of his role:

> To answer you, yes, my father is keeper of the prison and my mother is Matron. They did give me the post at £50 a year, but George, this is a House of Correction, where inspectors visit regularly. One has just made his visit and said I was very youthful for such a position [he was seventeen] which requires great moderation and command of temper…But he had no reason to suppose that the post was inadequately filled…

Young William had to cope with all kinds of problems, including something the inspector spotted:

> The parson caused quite a to do just before the inspector arrived. He likes to distribute tracts and books to the untried prisoners. The inspector looked through them and found a piece of secret writing and invisible ink. When he visited our hospital he found some of our prisoners experimenting with it.

The young man enforced silence with vigour. On one occasion, he grabbed a high-profile prisoner (who had been convicted after Chartist activity) and this led to a complaint: 'One morning as soon as I had left my cell the Governor's son took me by the collar and dragged me from where I stood and threw me with violence against the wall…'

The keeper, and all the staff, were learning that running a prison means constant whining and complaining, irritations and total vigilance. In a prisoner's mind the thought of freedom and escape always lies somewhere, even though that might be in the dark recesses, secondary to the aim of eating, drinking and resting. But the houses of correction had to produce and make profits. Staff knew that a harsh regime was essential, and it was tougher as the prison population expanded. Between 1820 and 1840 the number of prisoners almost doubled. In 1820 some 14,000 people had been tried for serious offences.

The local prisons were mainly established and reformed through the Regency years, and at that time, with over two hundred capital crimes on the statute books, war with Napoleon and government paranoia over sedition and rebellion in the streets, prisons were a focus of attention. It was in repression and fear that the unthinkable copycat revolution might happen, following events in France. To the keepers and magistrates, imposing forced labour and extreme punishments were the way to triumph over the criminal multitude.

The focus of the problem for the authorities was the ever-present threat of subversion from communication among prisoners. Through history and even today, that is still the greatest threat to the security of a prison population. Where today prisoners might illegally use mobile phones and can make phone calls to people outside using the normal landline phones, in the Regency years the threat was from any kind of communication at all. The governor of Cold Bath Fields prison in London, G. L. Chesterton, was drawn to support a newly conceived silent system imposed at Auburn prison in New York and reported on by William Crawford. This was a zero tolerance approach, based on the authorities' belief that any kind of group gathering or opportunity to discuss dissent was the first step towards riots in the streets. After all, in 1780, the Gordon Riots had shown what could happen if the mob took the chance to indulge in some anarchy in the streets. They had caused terrible damage in London, even the Fleet and King's Bench prisons had been ravaged in the rampage.

When governor G. L. Chesterton approached Cold Bath Fields prison in 1827 he was astonished: 'As the yard was approached, the ear was assailed with a discordant buzz of voices, occasional singing and whistling, and ever and anon an interjectional shriek.' He was soon to change all that. Later, when the Select Committee on Prisons and Houses of Correction reported on its findings, 'Entire separation, except during the hours of labour and religious worship is absolutely necessary for preventing contamination, and for a proper system of prison discipline silence be enforced…'

Chesterton, at Cold Bath Fields, wrote about the beginnings of the new rules: 'On the 29th December, 1834, a population of 914 prisoners were suddenly apprized that all communication by word, gesture or sign was prohibited and, without a murmur, or the least symptom of overt opposition, the silent system became the established rule of the prison.'

At any point in history, a prison regime will reflect the criminality and lawlessness of the time; in the 'long eighteenth century' the outstanding crimes were murder and other offences against the person, and damage to property. It was the age in which capitalism expanded and new businesses flourished. But the laissez-faire thought of the age of entrepreneurs also brings with it the need to protect property.

We know a lot about governor G. L. Chesterton because a French writer called Flora Tristan visited Cold Bath Fields prison in 1839 and met him. Her account of the governor shows how remarkable he was:

> The Governor, Mr Chesterton, is a very distinguished man; he speaks Spanish and French with equal facility…everything about him proclaims the man dedicated to the service of his fellow men. The prison is clearly the mainspring of his life and he regards the prisoners as his family; he knows nearly all of them by their first names.

Flora found his rules hard, though, saying, 'They prescribe rules of perpetual silence and solitary confinement for the slightest infraction.' Her explanation of the silent system is one of the clearest we have: 'Under no pretext may the prisoner address either his fellows or the warders. If a visitor ask him a question he must on no account reply; only when he is ill is he permitted to speak…Then he is immediately taken to the infirmary…any prisoner who breaks the silence is severely punished.'

The new conception emerging in the late eighteenth century of what a prison could be has the rule of silence at its centre. Jonas Hanway, a social commentator and thinker, summed up the new line of thought: 'Solitude in imprisonment, with proper profitable labour and a spare diet.' Christian beliefs percolated into the prison reform movement, and so it was believed that the right kind of imprisonment would lead the criminal back to the path of good behaviour and Christian morality. Silence was therefore intended to encourage reflection and soul-searching.

What became part of the prison establishment was the 'refractory cell'. In a report on Northallerton house of correction in 1837, it was noted that there were four refractory cells, one 12 by 5 feet and 12-feet high, and one much smaller, being only 7 by 5 feet and 11-feet high. The report stated that between 1 November 1835 and 1 November 1836 there had been 142 offences of talking, and 54 punishments of solitary confinement had been given. There was very little thought given to the consequences of imposing solitary confinement, and the opportunity for abuse – isolation as vengeance for instance – was always there. In 1836 one prisoner was confined in solitary for a total of fifteen days over a period of just two months for refusing to work on the treadwheel. The inspector made special mention of this case:

> During these confinements he refused food and his bread being given to him daily accumulated to a considerable quantity in his cell. The magistrates, the chaplain and the surgeon visited him but all entreaties were vain. The surgeon says, 'Every expedient was used to get him to take food, but without the least effect.' He was of a melancholic temperament and I am of the opinion that he would have starved himself to death if not released, which he was, after much apprehension, and he was subsequently employed in repairing prisoners' clothes.

As explained in the previous chapter, silence and solitary confinement went hand in hand, but silence as an integral part of the everyday routine was the aim.

Silence was a concept linked to what was formerly called 'contamination'. The early local prisons mixed men and women, remand and convicted prisoners, debtors and hardened criminals. There was separation to a large extent in cell arrangements, but throughout the day's regime there was every opportunity to talk. That talk would often be of criminal matters of course, and there has always been a 'school of crime' in a prison population. Against the silent-system idea were the separatists, those who saw that talk within isolated groups was much less of a problem, so that first offenders, for instance, should not mix with recidivists.

Auburn prison in New York state had pioneered the silent system; it was labour intensive, in that prison staff had to be vigilant all through the working day, pouncing on any small-talk while labour was in progress. Auburn had been built in 1816, and from the start it was revolutionary in its operation: convicts slept in individual cells and silence was enforced at all times of the day. This system came from the earlier Pennsylvania system in which prisoners were locked up in individual cells for twenty-four hours a day – even working in their cells. Auburn tried that method in 1821, but the result was that a large proportion of the men suffered severe mental illness after the experiment.

At Auburn other methods of imposing a back-up system to a rule of silence were invented, notably in movements such as the 'lock step', which was a human chain idea, each man holding the clothes of the man in front. We can see in this thinking the kernel of what was to be the penitentiary idea, with a utilitarian notion of erasing the individual and making the community function in economic and rationalized ways.

These ideas were soon part of the British system, and at the remand stage there was still separation, as in this ruling from Maidstone prison: 'Prisoners committed for trial shall be divided into four separate classes to one of which a ward of twelve cells shall be attached solely for juvenile offenders. The others shall be classed accordingly to character and conduct as well as to the nature of the charges on which they are committed.'

The rule of silence had to be enforced by severe punishments. The gaolers' journals across the country are packed with these types of entries: 'Confined Joseph Bailey in the dark cells for talking' and 'Confined Henry Oakes to his room for using thretnin [sic] prophane [sic] and abusive language to myself and Millin, the turnkey.' Women endured the same rough treatment, as in the case of Mary Burrell in Maidstone: 'Confined to dark cell for three days on the report that she has used improper language.'

Reports on 'association' of prisoners – a term still used today –

responded to the need for vigilance on the part of the staff, and in fact the records of prisons at this time are actually intelligence reports, because association meant potential trouble – even plans to damage property or attempt an escape. Association by day and by night was the subject of many reports, as in this:

> The prisoners work in gangs of about twelve to twenty on treading wheels, at the capstan and in the manufactory…at night nearly the whole of the male population sleep in separate cells…The females work from eight to ten together in the wash-house and in gangs together on the treading-wheels. There are eighteen cells in which the females sleep single, the remainder sleep in cells with two or three others. The whole of the prisoners are under the constant supervision of the officers of the prison.

The separate system won the day eventually. It came as part of the new concept of the penitentiary and the new regime meant that isolation was enforced even in movement, and anonymity; the latter was enforced by use of the 'Scottish cap' – a hat similar to a baseball cap, with slits for the eyes and a mask to cover the face. At all times out of cells the caps had to be worn; even at religious services, pews in chapel were separated into individual cells.

The first penitentiary was built at Millbank and stood where the Tate Gallery now stands. It had three miles of corridors and 1,000 cells; it was a convict prison, and the inmates were forbidden to talk to each other for the period of the first half of their sentence.

The concept of the giant penitentiary we owe to the philosopher Jeremy Bentham, who conceived of what he called the 'Panopticon'. This literally means 'seeing everything' and the plan was to have a prison with radial wings emanating from a central viewing-place. The Victorian prisons still in our current system all have this radial design, but the penitentiary was on a much grander scale.

Bentham proposed this in opposition to the expanding operation of transportation to the new Australian colonies after the loss of the American colonies after the War of Independence of 1777. He saw the use of transportation as a wrong move, and that large-scale prisons at home would solve the problem of prison over-population, much as Titan prison was put forward in 2008 to remedy the same problem. Bentham battled long and hard for his Panopticon to be created and he finally abandoned it by 1820, but Millbank was created as an experiment. The first forty prisoners arrived on 26 June 1816, after being carried in vans and chained together, from Newgate to Blackfriars Bridge, where they were put on board a barge and taken under police guard to the new prison.

Penitentiaries were not new: there had been a Penitentiary Act in 1779, as explained earlier, thanks to the work of John Howard and others. That Act merely made state prisons a possibility, though the plan was long term. Much of the Enlightenment thinking, as expressed by Howard and Romilly, was put into practice: the work was tough but there was pay; religion was integrated into the regime, and reforming the individual was the priority. The governor was also the chaplain in 1837. This was Daniel Nihil, appointed by the inspector, a Reverend Whitworth Russell.

Nihil was severe and unflinching; he believed in harsh discipline and a firm belief in demanding physical work. Although this new national prison was supervised by a committee, Nihil was the master. Even his name suggests an irony, being Latin for 'nothing'. It was certainly hard to get anything out of him. At one time he was challenged with evidence that the strong insistence on separation at all times was having a detrimental effect on the sanity of prisoners, and his response was, 'What I object to is a nominal separation accompanied with secret fraudulent communication. Health is certainly a consideration, but are morals less?'

Nihil's regime included the scandal of three little girl prisoners who had been in solitary confinement for a year, but 1822–3 was surely the *annus horribilis* of the penitentiary. The governor at that time was John Couch. In September 1822, two convicts, Edward Chubb and Elizabeth Collis, died in the prison and at the coroner's inquest it was decided that Chubb, who had had a 'scrofulous infection of the neck', and Collis, who had suffered from tuberculosis, died of natural causes. But just one month later there was a similar inquest on the death of teenager Jane Downes, and the surgeon, Dr

Hutchinson, gave a long and garbled account of his treatment of her, including the admission that she had 'fallen down' at one point. He was not convincing, and questions were asked as to whether the girl was assaulted. Eventually a verdict of 'visitation by God' was decided on, as the doctor could give no explanation.

Then, six months later, the doctor was dismissed from his post. It seems that he was not culpable, as the too frequent deaths and illnesses were due to a lack of proper food. The doctor had tried to fight the committee on the matter and had failed. His friend Morton Pitt wrote on the subject: 'I have often lamented the jealousies and cabals amongst the officers which from an early period have been so prevalent at the penitentiary' and he claimed that 'Too much detail has been undertaken by the committee and in point of fact they have been *governing...*'

Soon after, the worst event occurred: a truly dreadful inquest into the death of a girl prisoner. *The Times* reported: 'The jury, being sworn, adjourned to view the body, which was reduced to a mere skeleton, but bore the relics of a once very pretty woman.' The surgeon and governor were questioned, and at one point this interchange took place:

> *Juror*: What quantum of meat is allowed per day? [*Reply*: Six ounces.]
> *Coroner*: Gentlemen, I don't know if you are aware that several acts of parliament are made for the better regulation of the penitentiary...
> *Juror*: All we want to know is whether the meat be good and I should like the Governor to produce a sample.

No sample was produced.

The whole sorry saga of Millbank led to the scurvy scandal of 1823 (the press reported that '400 unhappy wretches are now in the infirmary') and the prison was cleared, the women pardoned, and others sent to the hulks. The first penitentiary had failed. There had been endless tales of violence coming from the place, typified by this story from a later writer who had been deputy governor:

> The Governor told the prisoners that the new brown bread would

have to be continued until the next meeting of the committee, where-upon many resisted when their cell doors were closed and others hammered loudly on the woodwork with their three-legged stools and this was accompanied by the most hideous yells…Four prisoners were especially refractory and entirely demolished the inner door and every item of furniture. One of them, Greenslade, assaulted the Governor with part of the door frame and I was compelled to knock down one of them, Michael Sheen…

The successor to Millbank was Pentonville, intended to provide a period of penitentiary life for convicts who would then be moved on to Australia. By that time, the penitentiary at Port Arthur had been established on 'Van Diemen's Land' (Tasmania).

Pentonville was referred to as 'the Model Prison' and again had a radial design, built on the Caledonian Road. It was opened in 1842, designed to take 520 prisoners, and using the separate system. Again, as with Millbank, the main casualty of the system was the human mind. Reports pointed out that instances of insanity ran at a high rate. Work and poor diet were partly responsible, and of course, with extreme limits on human communication, matters were made much worse.

One of the standard methods of work was the treadwheel, invented by William Cubitt, who installed the first wheel in Bury St Edmunds prison in 1819. He visited several other prisons after that, installing the treadwheels, as made clear in this note from Maidstone in 1824, 'Mr Cubitt having stated the tread mill to be ready for the employment of the prisoners, I this morning selected the numbers and placed them on the wheel at ten o'clock. Total 48. The whole of them have been orderly and attentive to their work…' The tread-wheel was adopted in the penitentiaries and was a gruelling physical challenge to maintain the constant steps to move the giant wheel. They were used to drive machinery, at first to grind corn. Images of treadwheels give conflicting suggestions about discipline. Some pictures show men reading on the bench during their short rest period, whereas some accounts suggest that there was no activity allowed during the work period.

One of the best accounts of the treadwheel is from James Burnley, who visited the Wakefield prison in 1870:

> A small engine is kept running with the wheels, as a sort of steadying power, but round and round the wheels go with a terribly persistent monotony. This work is given as punishment for breaking regulations and it is so hard that only those men whom the doctor certifies as of first-class physical capabilities can be put to it. A grim warder stands over them, watching every step they take. The front of the wheel is boxed off into compartments, each admitting one treader at a time, so that not only is a man unable to speak to, but he is unable to see, any of his fellows...

The treadwheel could and did cause problems, along with other prison work such as picking oakum and sewing mail bags. One reason for this was that some prisoners saw themselves as political prisoners rather than common criminals and so argued that they should not work. The Chartists of the 1830s often had this attitude, as was the case with William Martin of Sheffield, who was imprisoned after Chartist disturbances in 1840. He caused the governor, William Shepherd, some problems concerning this issue. He was forced to work on the treadwheel and he told inspectors what had happened: 'One morning, as soon as I left my cell he took me by the collar...he told me I must expect different treatment from what I received in York and he added that men had been reduced to mere skeletons when their term of imprisonment expired and that would be the case with me...'

The issue of political prisoners and the treadwheel was even discussed in Parliament but it achieved nothing. In Pentonville it was a standard part of the regime. Punishments were severe and sometimes they were corporal, such as the use of the 'cat' – the lash applied to the bare back. In Reading prison, for instance, one record book notes, 'James Crew (16) for repeated offences against discipline received 12 lashes of the birch' and 'John Bowler awarded 25 strokes of the cat for irreverent behaviour in chapel'.

But there were dissenting voices about the separate system. The chaplain of Pentonville wrote that 'Separate confinement is no panacea for criminal depravity. It has been supposed capable of reforming a man from habits of theft to a life of honesty, from vice to virtue. It has no such power. No human punishment has ever done this.' But these voices were few. On the whole, repression and savage punishment were the order of the day. Rehabilitation was considered to be possible from the enforced silent and spiritual reflections inside the prison walls.

The penitentiary regime was backed up by the lash as well as other punishments. The extreme punishment of the cat was standard fare in the armed forces. In 1817, a soldier died after being lashed for stealing a spoon from the officers' mess. The usual object used was the 'cat o' nine tails' – a leather whip with several strands so that several parallel wounds would be inflicted with each swing of the whip. This was used in adult convict prisons, and some of the most horrendous examples are from the penal colonies and from the home prisons – more frequently when they came under quasi-military rule later in the nineteenth century, as will be discussed in the next chapter. The convict prisons and distant penitentiaries were to bring their own cruelties, and the words 'Van Diemen's Land' were enough to cause a shiver of fear in men awaiting their journey across the oceans to the prison colonies. Across what is present-day Tasmania, the prisons had their yards and lashing frames, created as a normal part of the design and furniture of the buildings.

The silent and separate systems, then, were effective in terms of the prison regime as conceived in the first local prisons and penitentiaries; the real consequences of that approach were not really understood until much later, though, in the early twentieth century.

5

Hard Labour and the Lash

The infernal machine was 3 feet 6 inches high by 2 feet wide; it had strong steel joints and a brass pulley. Inside was a cistern of strong copper, a valve and a rod loaded with a lever and weight. Attached was a gyrometer to record how many revolutions of the handle had been effected. The man using this had to stand on a wooden step and turn the handle between 20,000 and 25,000 times a day during his prison life.

This machine was the crank, available to prisons from 1840 and destined to be known by inmates as 'the screw' – a term later transferred to apply to warders. Even today, the prison officer is still known inside the walls as the 'screw'.

Turning the crank was, of course, non-productive labour and so was deeply hated and resented. In some prisons, punishment was meted out for not working on the crank to a sufficient number of turns. In Leicester, for instance, the governor set the number of turns and by 1850 there were thirty-three cranks there; to have his meal, a prisoner had to turn the crank, so that 1,800 turns earned him his breakfast and 4,500 turns earned him his dinner. A Select Committee of 1850 approved of the system, and they noted in their report: 'That hard labour is not compatible with individual situation, and that where they have been tried in combination, as at Leicester, the effect has been remarkable in the decrease in the number of criminals.' But elsewhere the system was condemned, as in a report of 1852 which had a comment that this was 'a revolting and ineffectual discipline'. One inspector said that this was 'unwarranted by the law of England'.

At Leicester, poor performance at the crank meant that the man was reported to the governor for 'idleness' and 'obstinacy'. If there was a second report, there was no meal for the transgressor. This was not stopped until 1852. The Royal Commission just before that reported on interviews with prisoners and quoted this from one man: 'That work at the crank was so severe that when I was in the middle of it I tried to break my arm. I should not have cared if I had broken my neck. I tried to break my arm across the machine.' The inspectors said that the repercussions of crank work on health were dire and extremely detrimental to mental and physical well-being. They referred to loss of weight, sweating to extremes, and a swelling of the legs that became known as 'crank oedema'.

This was just one of the array of tortures in the prison regime

THE GRAPHIC, 1873

Prisoners at work in Newgate. This picture shows the tedious and regulated labour in Victorian prisons, with poor light and long hours.

known as 'hard labour'. There had always been hard labour in the
houses of correction and in many local prisons, but from the 1840s
through to the 1877 nationalization of the prisons, the demanding
work carried out in them was mostly a mix of the crank, the treadwheel, lifting shot (cannon balls) and picking oakum. Added to that
could be any kind of labour. Prisoners had different classifications,

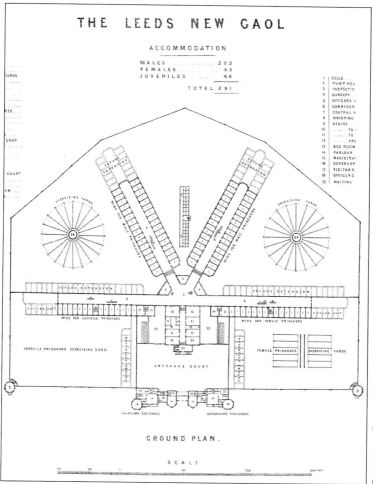

Leeds New Gaol. This was one of the first city gaols built at the time of the first
reforms in the 1850s.

PARLIAMENTARY PAPERS, 1855

and the work they did depended on their status. The dietary also related to the classification, and of course male and female dietaries were different. As explained in the last chapter, the treadwheel was the main instrument of hard graft in the prison. In Stafford prison, for instance, there were eight treadwheels used in 1883. The cranks were usually in the cells, but some prisons had crank sheds for cripples to use – those not capable of using the treadwheel. Oakum picking was for women or for weaker prisoners, or even juveniles, but men, after working on the treadwheel, would also transfer to the oakum-picking room. Oakum picking was the chore of unravelling old, tarred ropes to make new fibres which could be used to caulk ships' fabric.

Basically, in the mid-Victorian years, and through to the system led by Edmund Du Cane from the late 1870s, the prison ethos was founded on hard physical work, moral and religious reflection and severe punishment. The ethic of work was something profoundly embedded in the whole society, with Samuel Smiles's key work, *Self-Help* (1859), as a typical tract on that theme.

Paintings often depicted the dignity of labour, as in Ford Madox Brown's picture called 'Work' (1865), in which God-like labourers dig the road, observed by men in suits, including Thomas Carlyle, who played his part in writing eulogies to self-help and the work ethic.

Work and physical punishment were central to everything. Although there were nasty punishments such as the gag – which was a piece of iron over the tongue and a head-dress fitted, adorned with a red feather – the lash was the most feared. Mentioned briefly in the last chapter, flogging needs to be explained further. As well as being something that would inflict horrendous pain to the man being punished, it was also meant to put fear into the hearts of all who heard or saw the cat o' nine tails being administered. In Reading prison, in 1897, Oscar Wilde was so horrified by the lash that he wrote a letter to *The Daily Chronicle*:

> On Saturday week last I was in my cell at about 1 o'clock occupied cleaning...suddenly I was startled by the prison silence being broken

by the most horrible and revolting shrieks, or rather howls, for at first
I thought an animal like a bull or a cow was being unskilfully slaugh-
tered outside the prison walls. I soon realised, however, the howls
proceeded from the basement of the prison, and I knew that some
wretched man was being flogged…the next day I saw the poor fellow
at exercise, his weak, ugly, wretched face bloated by tears and hysteria
almost beyond recognition.

As has already been noted, flogging and whipping were standard
practice in the army and navy, but use of the whip or cat went back
a very long way in the British criminal justice system. At quarter
sessions, magistrates often sentenced prisoners to whipping and
branding, as well as to time in the stocks and pillory. In 1645, William
Finch pleaded guilty to stealing a saddle. He was convicted of petty
larceny and he was 'to be whipped and then delivered'. In other
words, he had already spent several months rotting in a prison, and
then he was whipped and released.

Until the mid-nineteenth century, offenders were whipped, but
there was no strict regulation on usage and number of lashes; women
were whipped until 1820 and public flogging was practised until the
1830s. In previous centuries, one of the duties of the town hangman
was to whip offenders 'at the cart's tail'. It was even used outside of
prison, as a direct corporal punishment, but with several moral difficulties attached, as this report from *The Inverness Journal* for 1817
shows, after a woman called Grant had been flogged through the
streets of the town for 'intoxication and bad behaviour' and reporters
had noted 'public and repeated flagellation on the naked body of a
woman is revolting to our general ideas of decency and humanity':

> We doubt whether such an exhibition is calculated to amend our
> morals: on the unfortunate object in question (a young and handsome
> woman) the hardened and indifferent audacity with which she bore
> and ridiculed the punishment, showed that it failed of that effect – so
> much indeed, notwithstanding this third flagellation, we understand
> that she returned from her banishment the same evening…

When used by the prison authorities and the military, there were no such qualms or moral dilemmas – the cat o' nine tails was the instrument of pain used. However, in the 1860s its use was restricted, and the birch was to be used on juveniles.

In prison, the cat o' nine tails, a multi-tailed whip made of knotted thongs around two and a half feet long, designed to lacerate the skin, was used frequently. The nine tails are the ends of the plaited ropes. These are made by weaving together three ropes. Prisons had a flogging frame that was used for flogging; the frame was a huge x-shape of wood with a thick pad across the centre and foot-straps down at the lowest level. There were straps also for the prisoner's wrists and the man's body would be held upright by two straps from the very top of the frame.

In some prisons it was used only rarely, but when it was applied, it clearly had an impact, as in a case from Hull prison in which a man called Bernard Hopkinson was flogged. He had escaped, with two

THE GRAPHIC, 1873

The flogging box at Newgate. Part of this could be folded into a 'box'. The frame above the box was used to tie the victim in place.

others, and after two days was recaptured. In a stretch of just five months he had breached prison discipline eighteen times, and it was decided that the most extreme corporal punishment should be applied. The press report describes what happened: 'An iron bedstead had been reared against a grating, and at the centre of it was placed a pillow, manacles being attached to the top and bottom. He was then led to the grating and securely fastened, his bare back being presented to the view of the flogger. Before this was done, all the refractory prisoners, being thirty one in number, were drawn up in a line.' These men were lectured by the governor on what could lead to this punishment. The doctor was present to check on developments; he was Dr Carnley, and he took Hopkinson's pulse before the first stroke of the cat was given. Then the governor shouted out 'One!' and the spines of the cat caused streaks of blood in lines across the man's bare back.

The man moaned aloud in agony as the next lashes struck him, two…three…four…His back turned purple. After fifteen lashes he went quiet, and then he was taken down and his jacket put back on him. His back was deep purple and yet there were no deep cuts, simply welts. But the idea was that he would never forget the ordeal.

It was, in fact, the first time the cat o' nine tails had been used in the prison.

Then there was the oakum picking mentioned earlier: work calculated to make boredom into a science. In 1862, Henry Mayhew and John Binny published a massive documentary survey called *The Criminal Prisons of London*, in which they describe oakum picking at Coldbath Fields house of correction. Three rooms were used for this unravelling of knots, and there was space for 500 men to work. The main room was very long, with a corrugated iron roof; eleven long rows of forms filled the place and there were six skylights above. Mayhew wrote, 'All we could see was a closely-packed mass of heads and pink faces of the criminals, and the officer keeps his eye rapidly moving in all directions…to see that no talking takes place.' Texts were printed on the walls: 'IT IS GOOD FOR A MAN THAT HE BEAR THE YOKE IN YOUTH' and 'GODLINESS WITH CONTENTMENT IS A GREAT GAIN'.

Mayhew commented that the men there were 'cowed by discipline' and that the place was a 'dumb asylum'. He noted that the silence was as 'intense and depressive as death itself'.

Regarding the work itself, if a man was not on hard labour, he only had to work with two pounds of bad rope; a man on hard labour had to cope with five pounds. Next to each man the pile of old rope was placed; some stretches of cut rope were white and some were coated in tar. The prisoner took a length and untwisted it, then loosened the mesh by sliding the rope backwards and forwards along his leg. After that a hook, fastened to the knees, was used to scrape off tar, and then the hemp was pulled out and ruffled like cotton wool. That completed the task.

If at the end of the day the weight of a man's oakum was not heavy enough, he was punished; officers walked with a big basket to collect finished work and if one was light, one warder called out the name and the other wrote it down in the punishment book.

The situation with juveniles was equally severe and repressive. In January 1889, a minor episode of shoplifting in Doncaster reached

ARTHUR GRIFFITHS, *THE CRIMINAL PRISONS OF LONDON*, 1890

An old method of employing convicts. This was 'hard labour' before the concept was officially defined.

the national newspapers and caused a lengthy debate. That may have been unusual for a Doncaster story, but the subject was certainly nothing new. The general public had been well informed about 'rings' of child thieves most famously by Charles Dickens in *Oliver Twist* back in 1838, and after that year there had been a constant fear of child criminals. The main statutory measures against the problem had been the establishment of the reformatories in the 1850s. That had been one way of dealing with juvenile crime – take the little villains away from home and work them into submission!

These tough measures had not really addressed the heart of the problem. If we accept that in the history of crime drink and poverty have always been causal factors, then that was central to the Victorians, and they had those problems in the absolute extreme. The massive demographic shift of labour into the new towns after the Enclosure Acts (accelerated after 1801) and the proliferation of the factories and mills had created a general need for child labour, and education had been slow to develop as a remedial measure – something to make childhood happy and, hopefully, imaginative. But it has to be said that the universal influence of beer shops and the habit of drinking gin at all times was a formative factor in making poverty a massive social issue.

The result was that the late Victorian years had new debates about children and the law. One of the most common features of this was the context of what we now try to deal with in issuing the ASBO: children left out to roam unattended, create trouble and fend for themselves.

This was the case in Doncaster at this time, and the story that reached the dignified pages of *The Times* was one featuring two children: a brother and sister called Margaret and Daniel Fell. They went on a stealing spree in Doncaster one day and stole two pounds from a confectioner in Hall Gate called Miss Brooks. That was quite a lot of money, but matters became more serious still when it was found that they had raided several other shops, averaging a few pounds in cash from each one.

The boy was ten and the girl seven; they had been taught to steal by a mysterious child called Harker, and of her there is nothing else known but her name. Margaret and Daniel took their booty and met another child, then all three decided to have a day out in Lincoln. There, they appear to have spent their takings, and not stolen anything; they went for a number of rides on the trams, and it was while on one of these that a driver became suspicious of them and called the police.

At the Doncaster Police Court, the children faced their punishment. The chief constable, Isaac Gregory, recounted the events of the day of the spree, and he said that their parents 'had a good deal of trouble with these children'. He told a familiar story: that the children were never supervised and the parents had no idea where they were; he said they were 'allowed to go prowling about at night'. It is surely unusual that the chief constable was there to speak. It is hardly a job for the senior police officer. Perhaps that tells us that this case was merely one of many similar ones and that juvenile crime was reaching mammoth proportions.

That appears to be the case when we consider the reaction to this crime. But what caused the heated response was the punishment. In Doncaster, the magistrate ordered Daniel Fell to receive 'six strokes from the birch rod', whereas Margaret received no punishment and was too young to be sent to a reformatory. The only additional action taken was that the parents (who bothered to turn up) were admonished and told to take better care of their children in future. A correspondent to *The Times* picked up the story and wrote:

> The reason why the real thief was dismissed scot-free and her less guilty brother whipped was, of course, not the one given by the magistrates…Had the girl been the child of one of the magistrates, there probably was not one of them who, when he got home, would not have given her a child's whipping.

The author of the letter was the Earl of Meath, and he was really making a point about the reformatories and the age at which young offenders could be sent to one of these institutions. From 1854 the ruling had been that only girls under the age of sixteen could be sent to a reformatory. For children such as Daniel and Margaret, the punishment was whipping and a caution. In earlier times, public humiliation had been the punishment, with the use of stocks and pillory, but in these supposedly more enlightened times, a beating was considered to be a civilized measure. As early as 1816 there had been a Parliamentary Committee to investigate juvenile crime, but little was done; children could still be sent to prisons along with adults of course, and this continued until the year following this hearing in Doncaster. Just thirteen years after these Doncaster children were in court – in 1902 – the first Borstal was established.

But the issue of fair punishment was still there at the time. The Earl of Meath was anonymously answered, via the newspaper, by 'a Board Master'. He argued that, 'I must join issue with him in his suggested remedy – viz., the substitution of the birch for the cane.' This schoolmaster was worried about the repercussions, saying of the birch, 'That instrument has hitherto been looked upon only as an adjunct to police courts, and its introduction into schools would, I fear, stir up popular clamour.'

In other words, the middle-class establishment figures, those with power to apply corporal punishment, had their limits and also their choices of suitable items of torture. It was all about a moral panic in 1889. The teacher wanted tough measures, and his statement on that opens up an insight into the depth of the public fear: 'The young men composing these bands of desperate, defiant law-breakers were shown at school what a fine thing it was to cheek the master, who could be summoned if he presumed to do aught but meekly endure it; and the disregard of the rule increased with their growth.'

The two Doncaster children lived at a time when there were serious social problems with gangs of youngsters, and their shoplifting spree opened up a 'can of worms'. The 1880s and 1890s saw a massive increase in the larger, more threatening gangs such as the Regents Park Gang, and in Liverpool the High Rip Gang. The fact that a day of shoplifting could lead to these significant national discussions is very informative about the state of affairs in this respect. The corporal punishment regime throughout society was not working; flogging in the armed forces was stopped only a few years before this case – in 1881 – and social historians have shown that corporal punishment within the family and in school continued until the 1960s in many areas.

Even sixty years later there were still debates and disagreements about juvenile crime, and in a sense this never goes away. In Liverpool, between 1949 and 1953, an experimental scheme involving visits by police to 39,000 homes, schools, youth clubs and churches was established, and had notable success in preventing crime.

In the early 1860s there was a virtual epidemic of a new method of assault: garotting. Up to 17 July 1862, there had been only fifteen robberies with violence in the city of London, but then an MP, one Hugh Pilkington, was 'garotted' in Pall Mall. A new and terrifying crime against the person had been noted.

In its chronicle of November 1862, the *Annual Register* reported that there had been a 'garotte terrorism' in London and in the provinces that year. The word 'garotte' was beginning to strike terror into ordinary people and newspapers were selling by virtue of headlines about this new version of street robbery. The report expresses the crime in this way:

> For some years past there have been occasional instances of 'garotte robberies' – a method of highway plunder, which consists in one ruffian seizing an unsuspecting traveller by the neck and crushing in his throat, while another simultaneously rifles his pocket; the scoundrels then decamp, leaving their victim on the ground writhing in agony...

The popular magazine *Punch* covered the menace with its usual acuteness and dash; one cartoon shows some middle-class theatregoers venturing out into the streets with a platoon of soldiers guarding them. It was nothing less than a reign of terror and it gradually became much more widespread than simply a hazard of London's theatre land.

This 'modern peril of the streets' was first described graphically as 'putting the hug on' and it had its own jargon, with the gang members having particular roles. First, there was the man called the *front stall*, a look-out; then there was the *back stall*, who would grab the booty; and finally came the *nasty man*, who would move in from behind to take the victim's throat. At the time, it was seen as a variety of crime that was somehow not 'British' and journalists tried to blame it on foreigners. It was often written about in terms linked to activities by Italian mobs. But soon it became clear that this heinous crime was becoming a speciality of the new criminal underclass of the expanding towns across Victorian England.

The terror even entered the realms of popular song, with lines such as:

> A gentleman's walking, perchance with a crutch
> he'll suddenly stagger and totter;
> don't think that the gentleman's taken too much
> he's unluckily met a garrotter…

In the provinces the new crime began to take hold towards late summer. The year 1862 was destined to become a proper *annus horribilis* for good people on the city streets, and northern towns were no exception. In Sheffield, one of the first notorious garotters outside London was Edward Hall, a man who was apprehended after a desperate struggle with police. It was reported at the time that he was 'the leader of a gang of ruffians who garotted and nearly murdered Mr Burnby, Earl Fitzwilliam's coal agent'. He was cornered and surrounded, then jumped from a high window in his home in Sheffield to escape. But in Birmingham he was grabbed and almost killed by a huge police officer who punched the villain relentlessly until he gave in.

In Bradford, the chief police officer, Frederick Granhan, was about to be busy with this new type of robbery and his constables' truncheons were going to be needed more than ever.

Characters like Hall began to appear in other parts of Yorkshire, and Bradford began to have its share of nasty street attacks by September of 1862. The streets of the city and the suburbs were indeed perilous at this time. A man was severely bitten by a dog in Grafton Street, and almost had his leg amputated. A fishmonger in

Keighley was robbed in broad daylight on his way back from a lunchtime tipple.

A more serious attack took place at Jerusalem in Thornton, where Joe Savile was set upon and robbed by two desperados who came across their victim at Well Heads. The attackers, James Jennings and William Shaw, showed no mercy; Jennings gripped the man's legs tightly while Shaw grabbed his neck, then they ripped his coat off. Somehow, Savile struggled free, and as he ran away the robbers shouted after him that they would catch him and 'kill him off'. Amazingly, though, the accused were acquitted because of a lack of clear accounts from witnesses.

Garotter gangs were not so lucky, and the full weight of the law fell on them. William Holes and James Lynas were in court for their garotte attack on William Dawson late on a Saturday night in Market Street. Dawson, an engine tenter, yelled for the police to help, and an officer came to the scene, to see the two robbers running away down Kirkgate. Holmes was trapped in an alley. Lynas was taken in Collier Gate by a detective called Milnes. They had taken a few shillings and a silk handkerchief. At York assizes they were to pay dearly for that attack, with a long prison sentence and hard labour waiting for them.

In Calverley, on the Yorkshire moors, a Mr Summerscales was taking his constitutional walk when he was set upon by two thugs called Elvidge and Hainsworth. They had used the established methods of one man behind to choke the victim while the other approached face to face, and they had stolen his silver watch. But on this occasion, the victim could not positively identify the men and they lived to attack again.

The press began to speculate about how the most likely recruits to the garotting craze were ticket-of-leave men. These were convicts whose terms of sentence had been lifted after good behaviour, so that they could go into society to work, though they were required to attend musters, just as today we have a licence system in the current penal code. A ticket could be granted after the prisoner had served at least three years. Penal servitude had replaced the use of the prison hulks in the Thames estuary after 1853, and men who had only served three years of a seven-year sentence could be released under this scheme. Ordinary folk started talking about all criminals as 'ticket of leave men'. The popular journals enjoyed creating this moral panic, making their readers envisage the local streets filling up with desperate and hardened criminals waiting to strangle them as they strolled to the Sunday bandstand concert.

All this led to the passing of the Garotters Act of 1863. In some quarters people raised a glass to the villains because their actions had managed to introduce extreme and repressive punishments back into the criminal law. In the prisons, garotters were in for a tough time. Two garotters were flogged in Newgate in 1871, and *The Illustrated Police News* reported on what happened to a villain named Regan who had committed a very nasty assault and who was about to be flogged by the national hangman, William Calcraft:

> Bernard Regan had been sentenced to thirty lashes, seven years penal servitude and seven years police supervision. The warders assist him to prepare: there was a good deal of the wild beast about his aspect, but he took it all very coolly, and in a few seconds the cross arms of the stocks were opened and closed upon his wrists, and the box-like lower part opened up on his wrists, admitting him and exposing the lower part of the body. Now Calcraft steps forward armed with a whip, whose handle is a couple of feet long and whose thongs – nine – are of stout whip-cord…The skin now goes furiously red, and the lines streaked across run into each other till by the time twenty lashes have been administered a broad scarlet band…marked the ruffian…

Punishments and restraints could take all kinds of forms, however, and in one of the most scandalous and repulsive instances of abuse and maltreatment in Victorian prisons was the regime of Lieutenant Austin and Dr Blount at Birmingham prison, which became the subject of a government enquiry in 1854. The commissioners reported in July that year. Mr Welsby, Captain Williams and Dr Baly wrote their report and a number of inhuman punishments at the prison came to light. They based their enquiry on the stipulation in the 1823 Gaol Act that although in common law a prisoner has no authority to punish (merely to restrain), some punishments were allowed: close confinement, and bread and water diet for no more than three days. Lieutenant Austin and Dr Blount had done far more than that, being fond of several cruelties in their regime.

Austin took over from a governor who had also been savage in his attitudes, a certain Captain Maconochie. These military men were used to running distant convict colonies in which they could rule as merciless tyrants and exact tough revenge on any prisoner who caused problems for them. Austin devised his special item of terror: the 'punishment jacket'. *The Times* explained what this was: '…a straight waistcoat with a rigid leather stock or collar, the prisoner generally being strapped to the wall of his cell in a standing posture, by tight straps which drew back the arms and kept them in a painful position'.

At Birmingham, among the sad cases of abuse the one that stood out was the sorry suicide of Edward Andrews, who was only fifteen. He was committed to hard labour, despite the fact that he was 'a very ignorant poor boy, very desolate in his circumstances, a mild, quiet boy'. He was put to the crank machine, and the report explains what happened:

> He was deficient in his task the first two days, and therefore fed on bread and water, not receiving it till night. A fortnight afterwards, being lazy and breaking the index of the crank, he was put into the punishment jacket for four or five hours, with bread and water. The same treatment was repeated two days after…

Young Andrews was seen by the chaplain, and he 'wailed piteously' to him. But he was then in such an extremely agitated state that he swore, and once more he was in the jacket. He carried on making trouble; he managed somehow to break his crank machine and also talked to another boy. The result was he was reported to the justices, who could, he was threatened, order him to be put in solitary for a month. His next action was to hang himself. The chaplain was certain that the pains of hunger and the mental anguish led him to take the only route he could to end the torture.

It was not an isolated example of the Austin regime. The commissioners inspected the punishment jacket, and they explained that it compressed the chest most painfully; one man said that in the awful thing, he felt that his heart was crushed. The jacket was sometimes kept on all night, and in one case a prisoner who was clearly insane shouted when the jacket was put on. This brought Dr Blount into the reckoning – another sadist. His favourite ploy was to pack salt into the mouth of a recalcitrant prisoner, and the poor mad man fuming at the fastening of the jacket had salt forced into him until he shut up.

One of the most disgusting cases of abuse at the prison was the horrendous treatment meted out to young Samuel Grey. He was admitted in October 1852, and at that time he was paralysed down his right side, suffering from the onset of consumption, was deaf and had a speech impediment, and it was also noted that he had a rupture. Yet this young man was made to run in the exercise yard. At the enquiry, warder Norton gave evidence:

> ...on the 18th November, when the prisoner was in the exercise ground, under the superintendence of the warder Jeffries, upon being ordered by him along with the rest of the prisoners, to exercise at the double, he tried to run, but had gone a little way when he fell down, and discharged a considerable quantity of blood from his mouth...

THE HULL DAILY MAIL

A cell at HMP Hull in 1909. The numbers in the picture refer to the comforts the prisoner might expect. 1 is a bed board, fastened down; 2 refers to a stool and table; 3 to a chamber pot; 4 to a ventilator, 5 is a rule card, and 6 a water tin.

The sadistic Dr Blount claimed that no complaint had ever been made to him about that prisoner. Samuel Grey died alone in his cell.

During the Austin regime, there were three suicides. One of the worst condemnations was, as the commissioners expressed it, related to treatment of ill prisoners: 'The infirmary was very little used; two men known to be ill were left to die, and did die, in their separate cells, with no human being present, and so did a third, who was partially insane, and whose death at the time might have been unexpected.'

Austin resigned when the enquiry was imminent and he fled abroad. As for Blount, he was hardly apologetic. He wrote to *The Times* to say that he had gone abroad too, and was residing in Paris, working on a translation of a work on insanity by a French doctor. At least, on that dull work, he could not harm anyone. From a safe distance, he added, 'I am desirous to meet any investigation

YOUNG OFFENDERS, YESTERDAY AND TODAY, 1928

HMP Birmingham, which was built to replace the earlier prison in which the scandal broke.

conducted as such proceedings are in our courts of law…these will remove those prejudices against me which followed the…commission in Birmingham.'

As an interesting footnote to the Blount story, William Dalrymple, a former prison doctor, wrote in *The British Medical Journal* in 2009 that while in that office, he went into a cell with an officer and the prisoner fell to the floor in an epileptic fit. 'Don't you do that in front of the doctor!' the officer said to the patient.

The hard labour was to be done on a very limited diet. Prisons used a basic framework of diets according to the class of the prisoner, so that, in Bodmin prison, for instance, around 1860, there were four diets for four classes: class 1 was for convicts for a term of over fourteen days, and they had gruel and bread all day, but on hard labour they had an extra four ounces of bread at dinner; class 2 was for terms of fourteen days to a month, and again there was bread and gruel; class 3, for short sentences of one to two months, allowed meat and potatoes on some days; and class 4, for long sentences, brought the best dietary which included more soup, vegetables and meat without bone.

It is something of a paradox that it was Disraeli's Conservatives who passed the 1877 Prisons Act and brought about centralization. Such policies were not entrenched in their manifesto, but it was an age of pragmatism in politics and all the sensible arguments were applied in the debate. It was the Home Secretary, Asheton Cross, who introduced the Bill for its first reading. His main contentions were that the prisons were expensive to manage and that the system was outdated, with too many small prisons on the list in the provinces. Behind the move was a basic political fact: the Conservatives had promised to reduce local rates, and taking the prisons into centralization was one way to do that.

Cross made an influential speech, with issues of waste and poor management along with a critique of the state of the prisons. There were opponents, of course; the main argument against was the same one that had been applied when other services were centralized – factories, education and so on. The voices against the move said that there would be incompetence, huge rises in running costs and that it was just not right to interfere with the principle of local government.

But the thought that at last a great deal of power would be taken from local magistrates pleased many; they were totally autonomous, and so that power was always going to be open to abuse. The Act would place the Home Secretary in control, and naturally he was a part of the functioning of Parliament. There were objections from the provinces: a petition from Nottingham was presented, and Oxford City Council complained, stating that they had only recently spent a very large sum of money on their establishment, and if it were to change then that would have been wasted. But after a debate on 12 July, the Bill became law.

The Secretary of State was now the person in command of the prison service. It was he who would appoint staff and he would have the powers previously in the hands of the justices; those powers

THE GRAPHIC, 1873

A soup kitchen at Newgate. This reflects the growing documentary interest by the public in prisoners' lives and also the dismal atmosphere of communal activity in prison.

applied to Acts, common law and to charters. Justices in their normal work were no longer to have any direct influence on prisons; visiting justices were to be in place, something that prefigured the later boards of visitors.

The new organization at the centre was the Prison Commission, with five Commissioners. The new body would have to make reports to Parliament and appoint the senior staff across the country. The first Commissioner was, of course, Sir Edmund Du Cane. It has been said about the man that he could boast that he could look at his watch at any time of the day and know exactly what any one of the prisoners in England would be doing. Du Cane was a product of the Royal Military Academy at Woolwich; he became a lieutenant in the Royal Engineers when he was only eighteen, and retired with the rank of major-general in 1887. He had worked in convict prisons in Western Australia, and his interest in the prison system grew

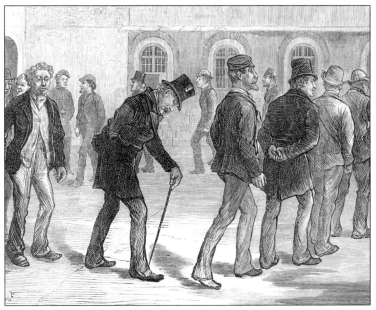

THE GRAPHIC, 1873

Prisoners at exercise in Newgate. This aimless physical exercise in the open air proved to be an inspiration to Van Gogh, who also drew this type of scene. The idea was partly to use this time as a roll call.

partly with his friendship with Sir Edward Henderson, Chief Commissioner of the Metropolitan Police. In 1863 he was appointed Director of Convict Prisons and Inspector of Military Prisons. He was knighted in 1877 when he took the job as Commissioner in the new prison system.

Du Cane held the belief that a criminal tendency is the basis of all mankind, and saw 'career criminals' as fools who were too weak ever to look into themselves and change; hence he rejected the religion-based attitudes of previous years. The task ahead in 1877 was to make prisons cost-effective and places so formidable that they would be a deterrent. He came up with a four-stage regime for the prisoner:

> Stage 1 (nine months) – held in absolute separation, and with six to ten hours of hard labour each day. He had no mattress for the first two weeks of the sentence and was allowed only religious books.
> Stage 2 – the work became less severe; he was allowed limited association and one library book per week.
> Stage 3 – a small release gratuity was in place and more books available.
> Stage 4 – he was now eligible for special employment and the release gratuity was raised.

As with all cost-cutting enterprises, places and people were dispensed with across the land: by the time of Du Cane's retirement in 1895, the number of local prisons had been reduced from 113 to 59. Yet within the new prisons and the reformed ones, the tough regimes went on, with a reinforcement of the hard labour when penal servitude was conceived and implemented in 1853 as an alternative to transportation. This created sentences ranging from three years to life, and was not abolished until 1948.

Edmund Du Cane described the penal servitude system:

> A sentence of penal servitude is divided into three stages. During the first, which endures for nine months, the prisoner passes his whole

time…in his cell, apart from all prisoners, working at some employ-ment. During the second he sleeps and has his meals in a separate cell, but works in association…The third period is that in which he is conditionally released…

In this may be seen the germ of our present system of a prisoner working through stages of a sentence by being moved through different categories of prison. But what was once hard labour is now more commonly working at a sewing machine to make T-shirts, or in a workshop constructing football nets.

6

Escapes, Mutinies and Riots

Such harsh regimes, tough punishments and brutalized treatment of prisoners had to lead to revolt, dissension and desperate violence. The psychology of a prison authority depends entirely on the imposition of security and the related concept of ruling by a show of power. Prisons have always had very large populations, and yet the few govern and command the many. To sustain this authority there have always been rituals, military discipline and the sheer appearance and presence of the warder. But at times, the inherent danger in the job expresses itself in a vicious rebellion.

In 1856, in Hastings Borough prison, an old keeper called Welland was strangled by a young prisoner called Murdoch. Superintendent Howse of K Division Metropolitan Police knew the offender; in fact, the police had a nickname for him – 'Bluey', because he wore old naval blue trousers. 'Murdoch' turned out to be one Joseph Williams, known by fellow criminals as Jonathan Wild, after the evil eighteenth-century thief-taker. He was in a gang of boy thieves around London, and turned 'thief-taker' after a robbery of £56 in gold, from a woman who had withdrawn the gold that day from the Bank of England. Williams turned informer and the thieves were apprehended and their 'Fagin' – a man called Jem the Lagger – was sentenced to fifteen years' transportation. Young Williams at that time had sworn to change his life, but now there he was in Hastings, a killer. After killing the prisoner he escaped, but was very soon recaptured and was later hanged.

As long as there have been prisons there have been escapes. Sometimes freedom is gained by corruption and bribery; sometimes sheer ingenuity is involved. Whatever the cause, the consequences are serious for the prison. Today, inmates in prisons wearing parti-coloured garb of blue and yellow are those who have attempted escape. The garish colours immediately alert any staff who have to deal with them.

Escapes of political prisoners are particularly irritating to authorities. In 1655, after the Penruddock uprising against Charles II, rebels were tried at the Chard assizes and sentenced to death. One man, Thomas Hunt, was going to be beheaded, but a memorandum book

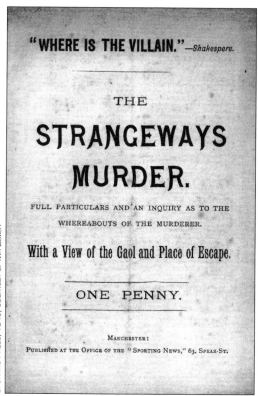

The story of the daring escape of Will Jackson from Strangeways, reproduced for a fascinated general public. Jackson was eventually arrested near Halifax.

compiled by the sheriff tells the story of what happened. First, the sheriff could not find an axe so he postponed the execution, and then two sisters came to see him:

> …two sisters came on the Wednesday night about ten of the clock at night; he shifted clothes with one of them (whilst two chamber fellows who lay at his bed's feet, went down to drink), went down with his other sister through the house, past two door-keepers and the guard of soldiers without, and so past away; but whether or how it could not be learned…

The remaining sister hung her brother's clothes on a hook and got into bed. The guards came, thought him asleep, and lay on their makeshift beds. His escape was not discovered until nine the next day. Hunt escaped, but the two sisters were confined in prison at Ilchester for two years and then bailed at Taunton assizes.

By the nineteenth century and the rise of the convict prison and the penitentiary, any dissension and unrest would naturally present a large-scale problem for the governor and staff. In 1861 at the Chatham convict prison, there was a riot. At the centre of the resentment and anger that boiled over was the question of remission: a new Transportation Act of 1857 had included provisos for remission, whereas those convicts who had been sentenced under the 1853 Transportation Act had no remission. As usual with riots and mutinies, a few leaders provoked action. There had been informers who gave warning to staff, but that did not affect anything. There was an investigation, and Sir Joshua Jebb, Inspector-General of Prisons, ordered forty-eight men to receive severe floggings, and 105 men were chained together, standing all day and night in the washhouse. Over four hundred men were confined to cells on a diet of bread and water.

A strong military force guarded a detachment of convicts who were sent to work on St Mary's Island, and *The Times* reported about the men in the dockyard: 'the conduct of the whole of whom has undergone considerable improvement, their demeanour presenting a marked contrast to their defiant behaviour a few weeks since…'

Mr Measor, the deputy governor, resigned after the outrage and, ironically, he had recently published a book on the administration of convict prisons.

At times, it was the prisons that had to cope with the insurgents who had rioted, as was the case in 1838 when a crowd of prisoners were sent to the prison at Cahir in Ireland. A woman had died at a farm in Knockgatton, Tipperary. At her funeral there was a mass riot as a crowd attacked and one woman had been dragged out of her house and severely beaten. In the end there had to be a military presence and extra police drafted in to help. An investigation revealed a family feud as the cause. What is not often accredited is how prisons coped when they received into their population gangs involved in feuds, vendettas and general malevolence. It still happens today, of course, and the only measure taken initially is separation. That means a large staff. We have to wonder how the house of correction in Cahir coped. Just seven years before this, James Payne had put forward a plan for a new house of correction there, but it was not enlarged until 1849. At the time the crowd of malefactors were taken there after the riot, it only had an accommodation of five cells, so we assume that the gang were bundled in a small space together as part of their punishment. There had been an escape in 1827 and the parapet around the exercise yards was duly raised.

Often, prisoners 'kicked off' over problems with the dietary, as they still do today periodically. In Newgate the Prison Committee once decided to change the bread by reducing its quality. On the first day this was issued, the prisoners refused to eat it and left the loaves outside their doors. There was then a service in the chapel and because there was an imminent visit from the Chancellor of the Exchequer and some female visitors, the governor sat in his pew with a loaded pistol by his side. The prisoners had brought their loaves to the chapel and they threw them from their pews, with the women shouting, 'Give us this day our daily bread!' The women were then removed. Later, one improvement was allowed: they were to have 'animal food', which meant a soup made of ox heads, one ox head per hundred people, and the soup was thickened with peas.

If trouble was not about bad food, it was often about sheer violent ill-will and overcrowding, as at the Liverpool Dock bridewell in 1819 when eight men were indicted for riot. They and a mob broke open the doors, released some people who were confined there, and assaulted some officers of the Dock Police. The eight leaders were sentenced to eighteen months in Preston house of correction, after using, the press reported, 'the most disgusting language against the bench'.

In earlier times, some local prisons were not exactly like the Bastille and escapes were fairly common. In Lancaster in 1760 for instance, a governor wrote this in his log after a break-out: 'Broke out of Lancaster Castle, by knocking down and dangerously wounding a turnkey…William Roughsedge, late of Prescot, in this county, by trade a shoemaker, about thirty years of age, broad set, middle sized, very black complexioned, a scar above his eye, several on his head, wide mouth and a remarkably rough voice…'

Daring escapes always have an exciting quality about them, and in the history of prison escapes, Jack Sheppard (1702–24) surely takes centre stage. He escaped from Newgate twice and he became a national celebrity, as is clear from this information in *The Newgate Calendar*:

> His short career provided employment for the bar, the pulpit and the stage. He was for a considerable time the principal subject of conversation in all ranks of society. A pantomime entertainment was brought forward at the royal theatre of Drury Lane, called Harlequin Sheppard, wherein his adventures, prison-breakings and other extraordinary escapes were represented.

Jack was a carpenter by trade, but he could not resist the temptation to rob the clients in their homes as he did the work. He then sold the stolen goods through a 'fence', but then he graduated to working with a gang and he came under the power of Jonathan Wild the 'thief taker' and he was informed on. In Newgate for the first time, waiting for execution, he escaped from the visiting room after cutting off a spike. But again he was given up to the law and found himself on his second spell in Newgate shackled.

There was something of the Houdini in Jack and he used a nail to free himself, then escaped by going up a chimney, still shackled. These irons were later removed by an apprentice shoemaker and he was free to rob yet again. He was eventually sent to Tyburn to hang, but even then he had conceived a plan: the victims were left to hang until dead, and he had friends ready to cut him down after a short time and revive him, but such was the ardour of his many female fans, that many of them tugged his legs to give him a quick death and, of course, they succeeded.

Such was the cultural impact of Jack that over a century later, when Richard Roberts was finally captured on the Isle of Man, he was called 'the modern Jack Sheppard' in the press. Roberts was first arrested in Ancoats, Manchester, on a charge of stealing four pigs, but he escaped from the police lock-ups and fled the country. He returned, and was arrested for stealing a firkin of butter near Preston, so he found himself in the Preston house of correction, but he then escaped, and on the Isle of Man he was put in confinement but escaped in the middle of the night. Two days later he was arrested once more, but escaped again; then, 12 miles from Douglas, he was tracked down. In September 1843 he stood before the magistrates at Manchester. Which prison he went to is not recorded, but the chances are that he escaped.

Sometimes sheer desperation drove a man to attempt an escape. In 1885 a man called George Mousley stood in Clerkenwell police court facing a charge of a breach of prison regulations. He was a stone-mason, and had been working on rendering some stone in the prison when he saw a chance of getting out and going home – where there were serious problems. He was working in a workshop, and he broke out of that by breaking stones around the iron grating while the warder was out of the room. Then he found an old scaffold-pole and with that he scaled two walls, one 12 feet and the other 20 feet high. He wrapped a piece of sacking around his neck to cover his convict number and jumped the 20 feet on to Guildford Street, but was seen by PC Bennett on protection duty outside the prison, who saw Mousley running along Farringdon Road and arrested him. Mousley told the magistrate: 'I am very sorry. I have been in such trouble about my home. The chance came all of a sudden into my head and I took it.' He went from there to the Old Bailey where he received additional 'time'.

Of all the prisons from which one might think escape was impossible, Dartmoor is surely the one most would think of. Anyone who does manage to get outside the walls then has to face the bleak moor; there is a huge expanse of heath and weather on Dartmoor can be far more perilous than a prison regime. One of the first recorded escapes was of a man called Brown who escaped into a blizzard and, after being brought back to prison, had to have his toes amputated due to frostbite. Escapees from that fortress were usually recaptured, as in the case of Morgan, who escaped by means of knotted blankets from his cell and then scaled the boundary wall with a scaffold pole. Armed search parties and mounted officers went after him, and he was caught near Chagford, some twelve miles away. Morgan had also escaped from Parkhurst earlier in his criminal career by breaking into the doctor's house and putting on some civilian clothes.

Some prisoners seemed to have the knack of escaping in the Jack Sheppard way. In the Victorian period, one of the most successful in that respect was Joseph Ralph, who was a noted robber and rogue throughout the county. He was given a sentence of twenty-one years' transportation for a burglary offence in 1854, but he escaped. The local paper described him as 'around thirty years old, with a full round face, flesh colour, and light brown hair with a tendency to curl'. He had been seen with his prison waistcoat still on, but he was on the loose and causing havoc.

Ralph had escaped by using the old trick of making up his bed as if there was a figure sleeping in it, and then slipped out. He was tracked down in Barton, where he was planning an escape across the Humber, and fought with a knife against two constables. He gashed an officer, Mr Jubb, badly on the arm.

Again, Ralph was put in irons in the castle, but he changed clothes with a lunatic prisoner and somehow had a replica key made, then, by using some of his bedclothes to make an effigy in his bed, he escaped. On the run, he stole from a house in Torksey – a butcher's smock he had taken was found in a field near Fenton. Eventually, at

Trent Bridge, he was cornered again by some officers, and after a fight in which he attacked them with some tongs, he was overpowered. He clearly had a wily turn of mind: he had robbed a bank in Grimsby by using several skeleton keys.

This time, Ralph was sent to Pentonville. But he was tried in Lincoln in 1855 and had a transportation sentence on him. One wonders if the forces of law in Australia were canny enough to hold him secure.

One of the most ingenious escapes in British prison history concerns Eamon de Valera, future President (*Taoiseach*) of Ireland. Before ending up in Lincoln, he had been put in Kilmainham prison after the Rising and there he expected to be shot, and wrote this note to Mother Gonzaga at Carysfort Convent in Blackrock, where he was a maths teacher: 'I have just been told that I will be shot for my part in the Rebellion. Just a parting line to thank you and all the sisters…for your unvarying kindness to me in the past…' But he was reprieved and lived to see the inside of several other prisons in his long career.

He escaped from Lincoln with two other men, John Milroy and John McGarry. The description given of Eamon de Valera says a lot about him: 'aged 35, a professor, standing 6ft 3ins and dressed in civilian clothes'. The report neatly summarized the fact that tracing the men was going to be virtually impossible, 'A close search has been made all over the city, but so far as was known at a late hour last evening the escaped prisoners had not been found.' They were not the only escapees from the Sinn Fein ranks: four men escaped from Usk prison the week before.

De Valera had been arrested in the 'round up' of May that year, stopped by detectives as he went home to Greystones in County Wicklow. He was then taken across the Irish Sea to Holyhead. The forecast by journalists at the time that he would make his way back to Dublin and 'arrange for a dramatic reappearance in Irish politics' was quite right.

How did they manage to escape? Lincoln prison fronts Greetwell Road, but behind at that time was merely open ground, beyond the rear exercise yards, and to the left, along the road heading out of

Lincoln, there were merely limekiln areas then. The escape was arranged so that full use could be made of the vulnerability at the rear. But having said that, there was constant supervision and, of course, they needed a master key.

A committee of Irishmen was set up to arrange the escape, and they selected a number of men to do the job. The focus was the small patch of ground used as the exercise yard; it was surrounded by barbed wire, armed warders watched in the daylight hours, and an army unit came to patrol at sunset. Sensibly, the first decision was to decide not to try a direct assault – a rush – as there would have been a gun fight. The next plan was to start by finding a way to communicate with de Valera. The answer was to use the Irish language. An Irish prisoner who was working on a garden plot in the prison sang a song, and the words gave de Valera details of the planned breakout. The second time a song was sung it was to direct de Valera to have an impression made of the key that would open the back gate. Today such methods would not be possible, but then there was more work outside and so there was a degree of vulnerability with regard to the system. According to one report, the key impression was made with the snatching of a key from a warder to press it into soap, but this seems very unlikely, given the fact that the key would be on a chain and always snapped into a belt-purse when not in use. Far more likely is the theory that a prison chaplain made the impression in soap or in a bread paste. The first two keys made did not fit anyway, and then the third model worked well.

The impression was wrapped in brown paper and thrown over the wall. Then came the hard part. De Valera would be able to walk through from the main prison building, but there were the sentries to consider. They would have to be distracted, and the way to do that was to use female allure. Two girls from Ireland were used, as the local girls may well have split on them. *The Lincolnshire Echo* reported that they were 'attractive, vivacious Irish girls, both university graduates, and they were directed to flirt with the guards'. On 3 February, four cars were sent around the country around Lincoln, to create decoys and keep the police occupied, then at dusk the Irish girls began to work on the guards. They lured them away from the prison recreation area and the Sinn Feiners then cut through the barbed wire and waited for de Valera to appear: he did, after some initial trouble. The key broke in the lock from the outside, as Michael Collins, who had come to lead the attack, tried to force it, but luckily de Valera, from the inside, managed to force it out.

They had to move very quickly, because Collins and Boland drove straight to the city railway station and caught a train to London. But de Valera and the others split and drove to Manchester.

Of all the ways of defeating the prison regime, the case of George Bidwell takes some beating. He was one of a gang of four Americans (his brother and a man called MacDonnell were the main elements) who committed a massive and very profitable fraud on the Bank of England. They were eventually tracked down and caught; first they tried to bribe a warder. As they languished in Newgate, the Bidwells and MacDonnell still tried to work their escape. They bribed a warder named Norton and he gathered some more corrupt allies from the prison staff. The plan was to have the Bidwells' brother John come across from America to organize an escape via a ship at Tilbury. There were to be guns involved and a rush out of the courtroom at the Old Bailey by the whole gang. But the city police were taking no chances. It is in this last act of the drama that the detective force is at its most impressive. John Bidwell was tailed by an officer as he went to an omnibus and on that journey the officer saw Bidwell meet and converse with the Newgate warder, Norton. It was clear that an escape plan was in process. The city officers were well prepared when the court resumed.

All it took was a nod – from George to brother John, and the police thwarted everything. What happened was that security in court the next day was at the highest level. There was a solid body of men acting as a police escort around the gang, and earlier eight armed policemen had trapped and arrested the warders. Chief superintendent Bowman was well in control. Two other warders had been shadowed going to John Bidwell's home, so intelligence was full and accurate. There was to be no escape.

As was reported at the time, 'The evidence for the prosecution was so conclusive that the counsel both for MacDonnell and for

George Bidwell declined to address the jury...' The summarizing comment from the reporter at *The Times* was 'Such is generally the end of all vast schemes of fraud. They need so long a strain of attention, that, sooner or later, some slight blunder is nearly sure to be committed by which the whole design is frustrated.'

Perhaps the most telling detail in the trial is the fact that MacDonnell translated the words of the proceedings into Greek as he sat in the dock. That men of such intellect could be criminal minds was a sign of the times, and was something that Arthur Conan Doyle would bear in mind in the creation of his arch-villain, Moriarty. Crimes in which the police were pitted against such fine minds in the service of crime were to be a feature of the whole process of crime investigation from that time onwards, being a factor in the creation of specialized police departments within the force.

But the tale of the Bidwell gang does not end there in its sensational narrative drive: after the savage sentence of penal servitude for life, there was a clamour for clemency. They were young men and they had not committed a violent crime, so for a crime against property rather than against the person to have such a draconian sentence attached was seen as too extreme to be allowed by some factions in society. However, the gang had committed the most outrageous fraud imaginable and had struck at the very heart of the British financial establishment. From the point of view of the City police, it had been a crime of huge proportions right at the centre of their 'patch' and was a source of profound embarrassment to them.

It was George Bidwell who stole the limelight again, at least as far as the media were concerned, and in terms of how this truly remarkable story survived and was retold through time. This was because he refused to do any labour at all after his arrival in Dartmoor. He said that he would not do one day's work for the Queen; a report of 1881 assessed his situation: 'Long disuse of his legs had reduced him almost to a cripple. The muscles were extremely wasted, both hip and knee joints were contracted...so that he lay doubled up in a bundle.' Through extreme ill health, he was released in 1881.

Finally, there was one other option of a kind of 'escape' for a prisoner: in the years before the national hangman Calcraft, there were more regional hangmen, and a prisoner could offer his services in exchange for freedom. One such prisoner turned executioner was known as 'Mutton Curry' as he had two convictions for sheep-stealing. Fate had been on his side because his death sentences had been commuted twice. He was waiting to be sent to Australia on the second occasion when he turned hangman. In fact, he was still a convicted felon, and was a prisoner as well as a hangman until 1814. Curry was to become a true local character – a man with a drink problem, and that comes as no surprise when we reflect on the nature of his work.

There had been no professional training of course. A man who turned executioner had no means of practising his trade other than a knowledge of butchery. If a man had been a farm worker, he would know about tying beasts and he would be skilled with a blade. He might also know a little about weights if he had used a pulley for grain in milling work. But he could only really learn by doing, and that is why, in the twentieth century after a more rigorous training was in place, dummies were used for drop practice. But in Curry's time it was an occupation with high-level stress and the gin bottle was very useful.

There is some confusion about Curry's real identity. His date of birth was around 1761, but that is not certain. He was from Romanby and his local thefts had led him into deep trouble, first in 1793 when he stole some sheep from an innkeeper at Northallerton, William Smith. Sheep-stealing was a capital offence, and the magistracy took a very serious and often inflexible attitude to that offence. But lady luck smiled on Curry: he was fortunate that his commutation for transportation did not happen; he was sent to the Woolwich hulks. That was obviously far from pleasant, but at least he was not on his way to a penal colony across the other side of the globe. Neverthe-less, Curry in his time on the prison ships would have had a very hard time; in the first thirty years in which these hulks were used, one in four convicts died. He would have spent much of his time lifting timber on the Thames shore and when he was not working he may well have suffered the fate of one young prisoner who told an enquiry that he had been in irons while working and sleeping and that he had worn the same clothes for two years. He had also been flogged, and one of the worst cases of abuse there was the case of an old man who had been flogged with a cat o' nine tails 36 times for being five minutes late for a roll-call.

But Curry emerged from that, and somehow returned, and then at York he took the chance of being the city hangman. What he was called has been a puzzle for historians; one writer gives his name as John; but he was reported as William in 1821 when there was a fairly substantial report on his work. A new drop behind the castle walls was made in 1802 and it seems that Curry did well, and in 1813 he was the man who hanged the Luddites, so he would come to be recognized. This was a high-profile affair: the machine-wreckers had attacked Rawfolds Mill near Bradford, and it had taken the military and indeed an informer to finally track them down. A new offence of taking at illegal oath was put on the statute book as a capital crime. No less than 14 felons were hanged at the first session and more were to follow.

Curry has to go down in the records as one of the most capable, because he handled this well and he did the work in two shifts, seven men at a time. *The York Courant* noted that, 'The spectators were not so numerous on the second occasion, owing to the time of the execution being altered from two o'clock to half past one. The entrance to the Castle and the place of execution were guarded by bodies of horse and foot soldiers.' The Luddites had conducted a reign of terror across the area spanning Huddersfield and Halifax, and even towards the Lancashire border. They had been fighting the introduction of mechanized shearing, displacing one of the most skilled trades in clothing manufacture.

Unfortunately, whatever his prowess and expertise before 1821, Curry will be remembered as the hangman who made a terrible hash of executing robber William Brown in that year. Curry had two execution appointments that day, and he had hanged the first victim at the Castle, and Brown was waiting for him at the City Prison after that. Curry was very tired by the time he reached the second place of execution, and he also 'took a drop' to steady himself. The local *Gazette* has this explanation: '...in proceeding from the County execution…to the place of execution for the City, he was recognized by the populace, who were posting with unsatiated appetites from one feast of death to another…they hustled and insulted the executioner to such a degree during the whole of his walk that he arrived nearly exhausted…'

Curry then had a few drinks to steel himself to the job; he decided to taunt and entertain the crowd by flapping the ropes around and saying, 'Some of you come up and I'll try it!' After that, he botched the hanging of Brown quite scandalously; as one report said, 'The executioner, in a bungling manner and with great difficulty placed the cap over the culprit's eyes and attempted several times to place the rope around his neck, but was unable…' He had prepared the rope too short. It was all becoming more than embarrassing – it was disgusting, though no doubt some of the callous and drunken crowd enjoyed it.

We tend to think of extreme barbarity and extreme sensual pleasure when we consider the media images of the Regency period. But there was plenty of humanitarian concern and conscience as well. In the same year that Curry was bungling at York, *The Manchester Guardian* reported on another hanging with the heading, 'Dreadful execution of our fellow creatures':

Before daylight on Tuesday morning a considerable concourse of people were assembled to witness the execution of three of our fellow creatures: Ann Norris, for a robbery at a dwelling house; Samuel Hayward, for a burglary at Somerstown, and Joseph South, a youth apparently about 17. There appeared in him a perfect resignation to his fate, which will be best appreciated by his own words: 'I am going to die, but I am not sorry for it – I am going out of a troublesome world.' The woman was (as usual) last; she seemed deeply affected. At 14 minutes past eight the drop fell, and they closed their earthly career. When will some mode of punishment be found to save these sacrifices of life?

7

Extreme Punishments

Usually, what is punishment is quite clear, and what is torture is a blurred concept. However, prison experience also may have elements of inflicted pain which are, paradoxically, neither of these. The classic example is what happened in British prisons during the campaigns of the Suffragettes.

In August 1892, a woman prisoner at Walton prison was brought to appear before the committee of prison visitors. She had tried to wreck what she could in her cell and assaulted the matron. Her punishment for this misdemeanour was to be shackled for four days, with her hands tied behind her back. The governor had directed the irons to be put on for a period without a limit, and that was his mistake. He was in the wrong. The case highlights the long history of brutal repression of women prisoners there.

Sidelights on history such as this make us wonder who committed the crimes in days long gone; another seventeen years after this incident, and again in Walton, there were events that make us ask the question again. This was what the Women's Social and Political Union was to call 'Atrocities in an English Prison' in their newsletter. The writers claimed that 'Two English women have been assaulted, knocked down, gagged, fed by force, kept for consecutive days and nights in irons.' The article was about Selina Martin and Leslie Hall who had been remanded in Walton for a week, bail being refused.

But the Suffragettes were to provide an even more sensational story in Liverpool, as a member of the top English aristocracy, Lady Constance Lytton, came up with a plan to be arrested and taken to Walton to experience and write about the kind of treatment that was being given to her fellow protesters for women's rights. Her father had been Viceroy of India, and her mother was at one time lady-in-waiting to Queen Victoria. Now here was Constance, a militant for the feminist cause, and she took on the identity of 'Jane Warton' when arrested in Liverpool. It was, from one point of view, an undercover job, an investigation, with herself as the subject of the 'atrocities' claimed.

Liverpool had not experienced a great deal of militancy over the period of activist campaigns; there would be only ten incidents in the city at one of the most energetic periods of unrest: 1913–14 – although Edith Rigby, a secretary of a branch of the WSPU (Women's Social and Political Union), did place a pipe bomb at the Liverpool Exchange Building in 1913. The bomb actually exploded. It didn't do the general debate any good at all that Rigby's husband approved of what she was doing. Such events helped to cause more division and mistrust, but on the positive side it made the men with more entrenched conservative views sit up and take notice.

Real militancy in the campaign had started in October 1905 when Annie Kenney and Christabel Pankhurst heckled the MP Sir Edward Grey. They went to prison for a week, after refusing to pay a fine. From then onwards, the WSPU had a militant 'wing'. Women in the regions were asked to participate more actively in local campaigns. Deputations to the House of Commons followed, and after 1909 the government began the 'force feeding' of women who were being held in Holloway. Then hundreds of women in all areas were held and force-fed.

'Jane Warton' was born. There is a photograph of her, showing a tallish, thin woman wearing a long black coat (with badges on the collar) and a large-brimmed hat to cast a dark shade over her face. It would have been hard to see the famous Lady Lytton under all of that. Lytton went to Walton prison where there was a crowd and, with the intention of being arrested, she committed her 'crime', as she describes it in her memoirs:

> I took to running and urging on the crowd…I began discharging my stones, not throwing them but limply dropping them over the hedge into the governor's garden. Two policemen then held me fast by the arms and marched me off to the police station.

Lytton explained the reason for going to Liverpool:

> I was sent…to join in working an anti-government campaign during a general election in 1910. Just before I went, there came the news of the barbarous ill treatment of Miss Selina Martin and Miss Leslie Hall…I heard too of another prisoner in Liverpool, Miss Bertha Brewster, who had been re-arrested after her release from prison, which she had done as a protest at being fed by force.

The conditions in the prison were harsh; she upset the authorities in lots of small ways, as in her attempt to combat the intense cold by wearing her skirt fastened around her neck. She wanted to speak to the governor when he made his first visit, but his windows had been broken in the protest outside, and he was in a bad mood. At least she had a gas-jet for some degree of light in that pokey, dark place, with its tiny high window.

Warton/Lytton refused food for four days when inside the prison; this meant that she would have to be force-fed, and her memoirs provide an account of what that was like: a gag was placed between her teeth, 'then he put a tube down' her throat, 'which seemed to me much too wide and was about four feet in length', she writes. This is what happened next:

> Then the food was poured in quickly; it made me sick a few seconds after it was down and the action of the sickness made my body and legs double up, but the wardresses instantly pressed back my head and the doctor leant on my knees. The horror of it was more than I can describe. I was sick over the doctor and wardresses, and it seemed a

long time before they took the tube out…

It was so horrendous that reports about attempts at resistance make painful reading: 'Force feeding was threatened so Mrs Martin barricaded her cell' is the kind of sentence often encountered in reading these records. As for Jane Warton, her identity was 'found out' and attitudes changed following a furore. The doctor, knowing who she really was, said, 'You are absolutely not fit for this kind of thing. How could your Union send a woman like you to do a thing of this kind?' What better evidence could the militants have than this? The implication was that it was quite acceptable to force feed and manacle working-class women, considered to be 'more robust'.

This issue, and the general consequences of the Jane Warton case, led to energetic leaders and letters in *The Times*. On 10 February 1910, the Home Secretary, Edward Troup, was forced to make a statement to the press. He wrote: 'I am directed by the Secretary of State to say that the statement that Lady Constance Lytton was released from Liverpool prison only when her identity was discovered was untrue. The release of "Jane Warton" was recommended by the medical officer…upon purely medical grounds.'

The facts are that Lytton was force-fed eight times. She had been entered in the prison books as having refused medical examination, so how could the medical officer's assessment have been made? The case had highlighted more than the different treatment given to militants of different classes: it also brought to the public attention the inhuman treatment of female prisoners that had been going on for decades, and in Liverpool some of the worst examples of this are on record. It was not illegal: the prison authorities were within the law, but it is a matter for debate regarding the justness of punishments such as shackling for many days at a time.

As for Constance Lytton, she died in 1923, after being handicapped by paralysis eleven years before. Her last days in Walton included an interview with the governor and the doctor: she said that they were 'courteous' on that occasion. Her courage was incredible, and her time in Walton not only highlighted some of the inhumane treatment that had been part of the prison system for years, but also the sanctioned attitudes and treatment meted out to women with startling callousness. Even the notorious death of Emily Davison under the king's horse in the 1913 Derby had seemingly not changed some of these attitudes to female suffrage.

Similar brutalities went on inside the walls of Mountjoy prison, Dublin, exacted on the women of the Irish Women's Franchise League. In 1912, the suffragist paper *The Irish Citizen* threatened a hunger strike in Mountjoy; the focus for this was Mrs Mary Leigh. She and some others had been given long sentences for trying to burn down the Theatre Royal on the night of Herbert Asquith's visit, and the *Irish Citizen* made clear its position on that act and its significance:

> The savage sentences inflicted on the convicted prisoners, cannot, of course, be allowed to stand. The judge himself was sufficiently ashamed of them to express the hope that they would speedily be revised by the proper authority…The Irish public must not fall behind the disagreeing jurymen in the appreciation of the political motive of Mrs. Leigh and her comrades. They must be accorded the full rights of political prisoners.

A hunger strike was planned. There was fury that Mrs Leigh had a term of five years to serve. The five years were of penal servitude as well – there was no stretch of knitting and sewing to be considered. By 3 September the force feeding had begun; on that date it was reported that Mrs Leigh was 'in a state of collapse'. A supporter, Mrs Grace Roe of Dublin, went to speak to the Lord Lieutenant about the matter. She was told that it was policy from England that was the cause: Asquith and Lloyd George wanted it done, and even Lord Aberdeen could not persuade them otherwise. The situation of the two women in question, Leigh and Miss Evans, was reported by *The Times* and the news was not good in the autumn of 1912, with the correspondent from Dublin writing that he had no reason to believe 'that Sir James Dougherty gave Miss Roe…absolutely no hope of the early release of the prisoners…'

By October, though, Leigh was released on compassionate grounds, but was facing trial for yet another offence. She had thrown a hatchet at John Redmond, a Home Rule supporter of Asquith, on that same occasion of Asquith's visit. Mr Justice Kenny announced that there would be a full investigation with regard to that second charge against her.

In December, the Cat and Mouse Act began to take effect on Leigh and Evans. In lawyer speak, they had 'failed to comply with the terms of their licence on release from Mountjoy'. They had not reported to police by the time set, and so they were to be returned to prison but were bailed pending an appeal to the King's Bench with the objection that they were not in fact obliged to report while on their licence.

We now return to the topic of what prison is for. Is it *as* punishment or *for* punishment? As described in my earlier chapters, the notion of prison being merely the beginning of further punishment has always been dominant in Britain. But there is a difference between punishment and torture. Torture was of course part of the everyday equipment in the Tower of London, but for the local prisons and the London prisons, it was considered to be alien to the English frame of mind: it was something that went on abroad, but the Briton was supposedly protected from the worst excesses of such brutality. However, this matter depends on how torture is defined.

Within criminal law, there had always been methods of punishment or execution that had elements of torture, in the sense that they involved a slow death or a prolonged period of suffering. A common example was the fate of anyone who did not plead when under a felony charge, as in the case of Richard Harris and John Pope in 1645, who were pressed to death because they refused to be tried. The most famous example of pressing to death is perhaps the story of Margaret Clitheroe of York. She was imprisoned for not attending services in Protestant churches, and in 1586 her home was ransacked by a group of men looking for a priest-hole. They found various items indicating that Catholic worship took place within her home and she was charged with harbouring Papists.

She rotted in York Castle until her trial, at which she was mocked and ridiculed before Judge Clinch asked her how she intended to plead. She replied, 'Having made no offence, I need no trial.' That statement led to what was known as *peine forte et dure* – being pressed to death. The sentence was delivered in these words:

> You must return from whence you came, and there, in the lowest part of the prison, be stripped naked, laid down, your back upon the ground, and so much weight laid on you as you are able to bear, and so continue three days without meat or drink except for a little barley bread on the day you do not drink, and puddle water on the day you do not eat, and on the third day be pressed to death, your hands and feet bound to posts and a sharp stone under your back…

Margaret walked to the Tollbooth in York and all of the above was done to her. She died after a weight of over 800 pounds was pressed on her. The body was thrown into a dunghill and later retrieved by a fellow Catholic. One of her hands is allegedly preserved in the Convent of the Institute of Mary in York.

Extreme punishments in Medieval and Reformation times went far beyond solitary confinement or flogging. The concepts of torture and punishment were often fused. In the most notorious prison for torture, the Tower of London, of course the patent purpose of torture was to extract confessions to crimes. Torture itself was illegal since Magna Carta in 1215, but it could be applied by special permission of king and council. Naturally, other reasons for applying torture existed within prisons, such as the necessity to find out where stolen goods were stashed or obtain evidence against some other accused person. When the Knights Templar were dissolved and tried at courts across Europe, the order from sovereigns was that they be tortured. But torture became part of the prison regime more widely in the Tudor period.

Discussing various tortures in detail is not within the scope of this present book, as punishment is the theme under review, but in some cases the punishment included elements of torture, as in the case of Guy Fawkes. Information had to be extracted from him about other conspirators, so he was tortured, but then his punishment consisted first of being 'hanged in chains' which meant that the man's fate was far more than being hanged by chains rather than by rope. The former keeper of the Jewel House at the Tower explains:

> When a prisoner is sentenced to be hanged in chains, he was first hanged in the ordinary way; that is, he was driven in a cart under the gallows, the noose was placed around his neck, and when all was ready the cart was driven away, leaving the culprit hanging. When life was extinct, the body was taken down, clothed in black, and tarred all over, face, head and hands included, as a rough preservative. The body was then placed upright in a closely fitting iron cage and thus suspended in some prominent situation in full view of all passers-by…

That is, some punishments went on even after death.

Prisoners detained after wars and rebellions were also subject to terrible punishments. One of the worst was simply neglect – which often led to death by starvation, as happened at York after the Welsh wars fought by Edward I. The king sent seventy-five Welsh hostages first to Nottingham Castle and then to the north, to be dispersed in smaller groups across northern castle dungeons. The prisoners in York were simply dropped into oblivion, and totally forgotten until William de Ormsby was finally commanded to deliver York prison. A patent roll summarizes what happened: '…it appears that when the King, by reason of the disturbance of the Welsh, superseded the holding of pleas by justices in eyre in the county of York many persons were…surrendered to York prison, where a great multitude died of hunger and the residue in custody remain in great danger of death'.

For more ordinary mortals in Medieval and Tudor times, the extreme punishments were mutilation. Many people had eyes plucked out or had their ears or tongues cut off. In the early sixteenth century a penalty for not attending church was having the ears cut off.

In the fourteenth century royal servants or fighting men could have their ears cut off; it was common for offenders to be sentenced to have their noses slit or their upper lips cut off.

If we have to record the application of gross corporal punishment, though, the place to look as we scan the years of penal inhumanity is the Marshalsea prison in the early eighteenth century and to the devilish handiwork of the prisoner, William Acton, described by Jerry White as 'A youngish man and a time-served butcher, so sufficiently strong and hard-hearted to slaughter the beasts, a man of courage with a cool head in a crisis.' He was also a disgusting sadist with a penchant for using his armoury of metallic devices designed to effect powerful restraint: the collar, the skull-cap, the sheers and a horrendous tool of agony that shackled head and legs in such a way that there was constant pain and no movement after its application.

To explain why and how these punishments were in use we have to describe the Marshalsea at the time: 1729, when a committee of MPs entered the prison to conduct an enquiry. Acton had the prison on a lease from John Darby, who was deputy marshal and keeper. As with the Fleet and the terror imposed by Bambridge, so in the Marshalsea, Acton was motivated by making as much profit as possible from his charges in the cells.

The debtors on the Master's Side were the ones with money and possessions, and debtors on that side paid rent: a huge sum of £555 a year. Fees were charged for all facilities, from a coffee house to the prison delivery fee. The Common Side debtors had nothing except charity, so that was where abuse and sometimes starvation took place. Acton made sure that charity sums from the City of London went into his pockets, and when the Oglethorpe enquiry finally looked into these abuses, they found out that large sums from charities had not been accounted for.

The Common Side garnered a reputation for extreme suppression and pain, and we know from a statement written by a former resident what the conditions were like:

> I had a very small matter with which to maintain myself in this miserable, unhappy place; yet when I was eating my morsel, so many eager eyes were fixed upon me, such a number of fellow prisoners constantly hovering about me, like so many shadows…without any the least subsistence…and daily seeing the dead bodies of others…I could not withhold from parting with some of that which was given me.

Acton's truly horrible, brutal nature is perhaps most visible in his treatment of Thomas Bliss, a prisoner who was himself not averse to extorting money from others weaker than himself. Bliss was beaten with a club, put in irons and, even worse, Acton put the sheers on him: these were double bars with shackles which prevented the legs from moving. Then the iron scull cap was put on him as well. This devilish device was placed over the head and then at the side it could be tightened by screws, so tightly that there would be blood forced out of all orifices. Not only was the cap screwed to his head, but he was also thrown into the 'strong room' – the lowest dungeon in the Fleet. He was left there to rot for three weeks and Acton used every painful device on him: the thumbscrew, and iron collar and leg irons. He was also shoved into a place called 'the hole', a small, solitary pit beneath the prison floor. Witnesses said later that Bliss's shackles were so severe and tight that, in one part, the irons could not be seen because his rotting flesh was 'overflowing' the irons.

The strong room was close to the sewer. There was no drain and no light reached there; at the trial, one man said that prisoners lay there on damp floors, by the side of corpses. There were rats and dung was dumped there. Bliss's major problems began when he was so desperate and half-starved that he tried to escape by throwing a rope over the wall. He failed and, after falling 20 feet on to the stone ground, he received his first beating.

Bliss was in utter misery, though was fortunate to eventually be released; but we know that he was a broken man, and died in St Thomas's Hospital soon after.

Acton's terrible regime was also monitored by an inmate called John Baptist Grano, who published *A Journal of My Life Inside the Marshalsea*; in this, Grano, a musician with a drink problem who sank into debt, actually records how he went to Acton to get help, and they dined and drank together. In this we see how Acton took all he could from every prisoner, beginning with appearing to be friendly (if they had resources) and then squeezing them for all they had. Grano's short notes on the horrors are most powerful, as in, 'A dead carcass was stopped for his living fees.' As Jerry White has explained, Acton also went out and about with Grano, all in the way of milking him for cash; if events were arranged at which Grano could play his trumpet, or mix with the artistic society of the city, then proceeds would go to Acton.

Acton was tried after the Prison Committee led by James Oglethorpe, which had reported that on the Common Side a typical victim of the regime would have this trajectory through his life there:

> When the miserable wretch hath worn out the charity of his friends, and consumed the money which he hath raised upon his clothes and bedding, and hath eaten his last allowance of provisions, he usually in a few days grows weak for want of food, with the symptoms of a hectic fever and when he is no longer able to stand, if he can raise three pence to pay the fee of the common nurse…he obtains the liberty of being carried into the sick ward and lingers on about a month or two…then dies.

Acton was acquitted: he had plenty of people to speak for him, and he was found not guilty on all charges.

Debtors across the land who suffered from horrible abuses and complaints were common everywhere. In Bodmin prison in the 1740s a debtor in the Sheriff's Ward wrote to the sheriff with an account of his own local version of the Acton type: 'The miserable manner that myself and my poor wife lie in for want of our bed hath almost killed us both…and to add to my other afflictions, Hawkey fell on me Saturday the eighth with blows, who am so infirm that I can scarce walk the prison…'

Matters regarding debtors and prison did not change until the County Courts Act of 1846 made the process and settlement of small debts smoother and less likely to end in a prison sentence, but it was not until the Bankruptcy Act of 1861 that bankrupts and debtors were not imprisoned. In August 1846, the new system of dealing with minor debt at the county courts was shown to be most effectual in the case of *Wood* v. *Rock*. Rock wanted the sum of £55 as a recovery of a debt from Wood, who had been a tenant of Guy's Hospital, living on some land called Buck's Castle in Hereford (so the case was heard at the Oxford circuit). When Rock wanted to buy the land, he had to negotiate with the Hospital steward, but he went ahead before matters were finalized and paid a £55 down-payment. When the purchase fell through, Wood refused to return the money, and so Rock brought a prosecution for debt against him.

In court, the result was that 'The counsel for the plaintiff proceeded to answer the learned gentleman's objections when HIS LORDSHIP intimated that there was sufficient evidence that the contract was rescinded by mutual consent.' Before the new legislation, Wood could easily have found himself in a debtors' prison for not returning the money.'

One aspect of punishments and deaths in prison that has to be explained is the fact that, in the many terrible regimes such as that of Acton at the Fleet, there were no coroners' inquests on the deaths. It has been the duty of coroners since 1194 to investigate the circumstances of unnatural, sudden or suspicious deaths and deaths in prison, and until 1926 all inquests were held before a jury.

Through the centuries, there have been times and places in which the normal process of a coroner investigating a suspicious death in custody has been suspended, or of course the inquest never happened because the death was not reported. Acton's charges' deaths were certainly not reported to a coroner. But the surviving records show that many prisons had coroners to certify and ascertain death and cause of death. Records of the inquests held at the King's Bench prison from 1746 survive – at least in part – and there are records of inquests for Millbank between 1848 and 1863. There are inquest records for the Fleet from the year 1783 through to 1839 (with some gaps) so clearly, after the Acton regime, and slowly, efforts were made to make sure that inquests were held on deaths in prison.

8

THE DEATH CELL AND THE NOOSE

Naturally, every prison at which executions were performed had its condemned cell. These spare, solemn places are sometimes today the focus of heritage trail visits, in museums or in the Victorian prisons that still survive. Typical of these is the death cell at the old prison inside Lincoln Castle. The visitor reaches this as the last space observed after a walk through the old wings and landings, the matron's room and the governor's office. It is small, plain and horribly unsettling to anyone who tries to imagine the thoughts of the fated occupants of that dismal hole.

Behind the old prison, after a steep climb, one finds the Lucy Tower. The visitor here will see a small graveyard inside the tower, with tiny slabs of markers for each grave, bearing the initials of the hanged felons, and a date – the year of their appointment with the hangman.

A similar aura of wonder and revulsion surrounds the death cell at York Castle prison, associated for ever with Dick Turpin now that the tourist attraction of 'The York Dungeons' is so widely known. York Castle came to dominate the criminal justice process of York-shire right up to the switch of the assizes to Leeds in 1864. The new prison was built between 1825 and 1835, with radiating wings and a governor's house. To York, for trial, imprisonment and sometimes execution, came the criminals of the Georgian and Victorian period. The long list of crimes and social changes related to the crimes covers such massive historical processes as the Luddite unrest of 1812–16, Chartist prisoners from the 1840s, everyday 'domestic' murderers, coiners, sheep-stealers, fraudsters and many others. There were poachers who had killed gamekeepers, sacked labourers who burned their masters' hayricks, insane people who took a knife or axe to a partner or companion, women poisoners and, perhaps most poignant of all, the young women who had committed the crime of 'child-murther' – until 1922, this was simply a version of murder, rather than the crime of manslaughter it became after that date.

Until 1801 the Tyburn tree, also known as the 'three-legged mare' on the Knavesmire, was the destination of these felons, from the infamous Dick Turpin in 1739 to the obscure drunks and men of violence; but after that date the hanging place was the 'New Drop' made at the south-west end of the assize courts, facing St George's Fields. The crowds that had once gathered on the Knavesmire to watch criminals die now filled St George's Fields to see the gruesome

THE GRAPHIC, 1873

The condemned cell at Newgate. These rooms were sparsely furnished, and warders sat through the night with those about to hang to prevent attempts at suicide.

spectacle – up until 1868 when public executions were abolished. The New Drop was first used on 28 August 1802, after the last man had been hanged on the Knavesmire, Edward Hughes in 1801. In 1805 a bank of earth was made that would enclose the scaffold, in order to keep spectators at a distance and avoid accidents through the crowds becoming unruly.

Other gallows gradually fell into disuse, such as the one at the city prison on Ouse Bridge, which had existed since 1578 and had been rebuilt in 1724. But in 1801 a new prison was made and this was to deal with capital offences committed within the city itself; some land near the Baile Hill was selected for this. The main outside wall fronted a lane leading from Skeldergate to Bishopshill Senior Church. Cromwell Road today is the site of this. When a hanging was about to take place, a scaffold was erected outside the wall by the Baile Hill and an opening was made in the wall for the condemned person to go through.

The Privy Council made the decision to move the West Riding assizes from York to Leeds in 1864 and York remained the county assizes for the East and North Ridings of Yorkshire. The City Prison in Prison Lane continued in use until 1869.

The backdrop to this long line of executions was the huge body of statutes embodying capital punishments in the criminal law of the land. By the year 1800 there were over two hundred such offences; in 1752 there was an Act passed that expressed the spirit of sheer inhuman suppression behind these laws; the wording explained what would happen to murderers condemned to the scaffold:

> Persons convicted of murder should be executed on the next day but one after their sentence of death has been passed, and that their bodies should be given to the surgeons to be anatomised, or hung in chains; and further, that the prisoners should be fed on bread and water only after being sentenced…

Dick Turpin is more myth than man. The basic facts are simple: he was born in 1705 and became an apprentice butcher; he began stealing and then joined a gang in Essex. He went into burglary as well, and when he was with the Gregory Gang in Essex this outfit began to strike terror into areas of that county. He had started out as a man whose knowledge of butchery made him useful in cattle stealing, and then progressed to some nasty criminal acts. With Gregory he robbed a farmhouse and there he poured boiling water over the owner (an old man) and raped a woman there. His image in contemporary terms was rarely glamorized: he was once depicted in a woodcut throwing an old lady on to a fire. His first murder was of a man called Tom Morris, a servant who recognized him as a robber.

Matters stepped up a gear in terms of his infamy and sheer brutality when he joined Tom King, another highway robber; but it seems that Turpin killed his accomplice during a botched robbery. He then fled north. After that he began to make a living horse-stealing, and to do this he stole horses in South Lincolnshire and took them up the Great North Road to sell in East Yorkshire. It was when the Yorkshire connection occurred that he assumed the name of John Palmer. But, as with so many criminals, he was caught after a trivial piece of business. His first incarceration was in the Beverley house of correction, and he was brought before magistrates in the Beverley Arms.

Palmer/Turpin was arrested for shooting a cockerel and the man involved in that incident was George Crowle, the man whose actions were to lead to Turpin being tried for murder at York. Crowle was the magistrate who was acting against 'Palmer' after he shot the cockerel, belonging to Francis Hall in Brough (where Palmer had settled). Crowle was also MP for Hull and he made sure that the trial would take place in York, rather than in London. Of course, what had happened to make everyone aware that Palmer was Turpin was that a letter was intercepted and his handwriting recognized. He faced charges of horse-stealing and murder.

James Smith and Edward Saward came from Essex to testify and Turpin was doomed. The judge asked if the accused knew any reason why the sentence of death should not be passed, and Turpin tried to come up with reasons to stay the trial. He even said, 'I am sure no man can say ill of me in Yorkshire.' But he was sentenced to hang and he took his last few steps in this world on the Knavesmire scaffold on 7 April 1739.

Even after death, though, his narrative continues with sensation and interest. His body was taken to the Blue Boar in Castlegate for public display, and then it was interred in St George's churchyard. But the doctors tried hard to obtain his body for dissection, as they were always desperate for corpses to use in anatomy classes. The mob were aware that the medical men had this intention and a pamphlet of the time gives an account of the populace supposedly saving the body from the doctors. A certain Marmaduke Palms was bound over for trying to take the corpse for anatomy purposes. In addition, men were charged with handling his body, as they had acted to protect it from Palms, a surgeon.

Finally, although it is not certain, there is a grave that is supposed to hold Turpin's remains at St George's churchyard: a pathetic and possibly sham final resting-place of this notorious villain, whose mythology was perhaps confirmed when Harrison Ainsworth published his novel of Turpin and Black Bess, *Rookwood* (1834).

Of his short time in York prison we know little, but Turpin spent some time in the Beverley house of correction before being taken to York. His death cell will always dominate the story for all visitors to the York prison, though. But the fact is that there were four death cells and John Howard, visiting the place in 1776, wrote that there were 'Four condemned rooms, about seven feet square. A sewer in one of the passages often makes these parts of the prison very offensive and I cannot say they are clean.'

According to William Knipe, writing in the 1860s, Turpin was quite unconcerned at the death sentence:

> Not many days before his execution, he purchased a new fustian frock and a pair of pumps in order to wear them at the time of his death; and on the day before he hired five poor men, at ten shillings each, to follow the cart as mourners. He also gave hatbands and gloves to several other persons...

The gaoler at York had made £100 – a huge sum of money then – by supplying Turpin and his visitors with liquor. The condemned who had any cash and resources had a strange final period on this earth:

sometimes praying with the chaplain and sometimes having a wild party with friends.

The condemned cell was a place of a very special atmosphere also. In 1860 Mayhew and Binny visited the 'murderers' cells' in Newgate:

> Leaving the male corridor we pass through an iron gate on the left into a small passage paved with slate…On turning to the left, towards the front of the prison, we came to two rooms reserved for murderers. Each of these is about the size of two common cells, and has an arched brick roof supported on iron girders. The wretched men confined in these are watched day and night by a warder. The furniture consists of a wooden bedstead about nine inches from the floor supplied with a mattress, three blankets, a pair of sheets and a pillow. It is lighted by an iron-grated window with fluted glass. The floor is laid with asphalt. A knife is not allowed them – the food being cut up into small pieces in the kitchen before it is brought to the prisoner – that is to prevent him laying violent hands on himself…

Often, in the classic narratives of the villains tried at the Old Bailey, the account of the condemned cell is full of the expectancy of a reprieve, and then, as in the case of the highwayman Sixteen-String Jack (Jack Rann) in 1774, the mood changes radically, and the death cell changes from a party atmosphere to solemnity, as this contemporary account makes clear:

> Rann was so confident of being acquitted, on his last trial, that he had ordered a genteel supper to be provided for a number of his particular friends and associates on the joyful occasion. Alas! What was the disappointment of the company when they heard the fate of the unhappy wretch – riot was turned into mourning, and the madness of guilty joy to the sullen melancholy of equally guilty grief…

The life of many prisons included the necessity of executing the condemned, and before the 1830s hangings were frequent. What is not so often discussed is the notion of exactly who would supervise and carry out the hanging. The public hangman was the target of hatred, derision and violence through the centuries in which Britain hanged its felons; he was also often made into a celebrity and was of course the subject of morbid fascination. Hangmen feature just as prominently in the exhibits at Madame Tussaud's Chamber of Horrors as villains. Even as long ago as 1601, they have been vilified, even by the men they hanged (in spite of being given money to beg that the death be quick). The Earl of Essex, executed in that year by the London hangman, Derrick, penned a ballad upon his life, and wrote:

> Derrick! Thou knowest, at stately Calais I saved
> Thy life, lost for a rape there done,
> Which thou thyself can testify –
> Thine own hand three and twenty hung...

The first hangmen were on the manors and in the towns, paid by both the civil and the religious power-bases, because courts proliferated and several categories of people in high society had the prerogative of hanging culprits in their domain. They were usually rogues themselves, as was the case with a London hangman observed by a diarist called Machyn in 1556, who noted that 'The 2nd day of July was rode into a cart five unto Tyburn [the hanging site near today's Marble Arch]. One was the hangman with the stump-leg – for theft. The which [sic] he had hanged many a man and quartered many, and had many a noble man and other...'

Of course, since capital punishment was abolished in Britain in 1964, we have become acutely aware of the adverse views of the act of hanging: notably the death of a person later proved innocent of the capital offence. Such was the recent case of Alfred Moore, a Huddersfield man who was hanged in 1951 for the murder of two police officers. *The Yorkshire Post* for 1 January 2008 announced:

> A former detective has uncovered evidence that casts doubts on a
> man's conviction for murdering two police officers more than fifty
> years ago...At his trial Moore, a poultry farmer with a lifestyle beyond

his legal income, admitted carrying out burglaries but said he was in bed at the time of the shootings. The murder weapon was never found.

Detective Steven Lawson had investigated the case and found strong evidence that the real killer was a local man who died in 1998.

In 1961 Leslie Hale wrote a book called *Hanged in Error* in which he looked again at eleven cases of executions for murder and argued that they were almost certainly executions of innocent people. In that book, Hale argued that there had been a period of complacency in which government refused to make any decision regarding the continuation of the death penalty, but that this attitude was shaken by the serious assault of a police officer in Marlow, Buckinghamshire, in October 1953. The officer was viciously attacked by a gang of three men, and he was so severely injured that it appeared that he was to die of the wounds inflicted. In early 1954 the men were tried, found guilty of attempted murder and given long sentences, including a stretch of ten years for one man. It was realized, of course, that if the officer had died, there would have been a hanging.

Then matters were complicated by the fact that the real attacker who had almost killed the officer was known, after a confession in custody. It was clear that an enquiry was called for and the Home Secretary gave the task to selected officers at Scotland Yard, and that enquiry proved that the sentenced men were, in fact, innocent.

Of course, whether innocent or guilty, the fact is that large numbers of people have been hanged, either at the London Tyburn or in the provinces, over the centuries, and their stories provide high drama, sensation and often darkly humorous entertainment. But the hangman in those dramas of the scaffold is often a shadowy figure, simply mentioned in passing. The name Dick Turpin is very well known in popular culture and history, but how many people know his executioner – Thomas Hadfield? He is prominent only if something goes badly wrong. Many of the hangmen of England have had a drink problem or been severely depressed or even notably unstable personalities; some took their own lives. On the other hand, some hangmen enjoyed their notoriety and took to the media or to travelling shows when their official careers were over.

The question of why felons were hanged is another that needs to be answered. Statistics indicate that hanging is not a deterrent, in the sense that the instances of murder do not decline in states in which there is capital punishment. Historically in England, the period with the most hangings, when the hangmen made good money from the deceased's clothes and payments for swift business at the block or gibbet, was the Tudor era. Between 1536 and 1553, approximately 560 people were put to death at Tyburn.

Hangings were a massively popular public event through the centuries, until 1868 when public executions were abolished. Thousands usually lined the route to Tyburn, and the swelling crowd at the death scene was often raucous, unruly and callous. In the famous

Cobb Hall, Lincoln Castle, where public hangings took place. This turret overlooks several pubs, and people paid good money to take a seat in a pub with a view of a death.

case of Courvoisier, who had murdered Lord William Russell in 1840, there was a crowd of 40,000 people waiting to see the villainous butler die. One of these was Charles Dickens, who described the scene and reflected on the nature of the hangman: 'I came away that morning with a disgust for murder, but it was for the murder I saw done…I can see Mr Ketch at this moment, with an easy air, taking the rope from his pocket; that I feel myself shamed and degraded at the brutal curiosity which took me to that spot…' Dickens used 'Mr Ketch' as that had become the generic name for the hangman by that time.

The public hangman's role and duties were eventually taken seriously by William Marwood, the Lincolnshire man who introduced the practice of the 'long drop'. Marwood practised with sacks in order to ascertain the right drop for a specific weight, such that a felon would die by asphyxia rather than strangulation. In many cases, in the earlier centuries of hanging, the knot was made arbitrarily, not by the requisite bone and artery for a quicker death. Though Marwood did have some memorable bunglings, these were not so common as errors made by his antecedents and indeed by some of his contemporaries.

Today, from a viewpoint over forty years after the end of hanging in Britain, it is easy to find accounts of the business of hanging – the procedure and the ritual – yet there is very little on the nature of the business of the staff involved. But in the official reports and enquiries it is possible to find sensitive and thoughtful writing on the topic. For instance, in the report of the committee looking into execution in 1953, we have these words on the hangman:

> At present, any person may apply to the Prison Commissioners to become an executioner…But we recommend that sheriffs should vary their selection of executioner so as to ensure that there are always two experienced executioners on the list…

The chronicles of hangings provide the historian with some truly horrendous tales. One of the most execrable examples of what happened when things went wrong comes from Liverpool in 1883.

Henry Dutton, an ironworker, had killed Hannah Henshaw, his wife's grandmother, and was due to be hanged in the precincts of Kirkdale prison on 3 December 1883. The problem was that the man charged with seeing him quickly into oblivion was Bartholomew Binns.

Binns was only in the office for a year, and was then sacked. Later, he assisted the more competent Tommy Scott in 1900, but in his own 'annus horribilis' as hangman he was responsible for a few botched jobs. He had helped the very professional and successful William Marwood, from Lincolnshire, who, as noted earlier, had invented the more humane 'long drop' method. But Binns did not learn much. There were several complaints from governors and clergy about Binns's work and he was politely asked to leave. He had a moment of notoriety when he was written about as the man who hanged one of the Phoenix Park murderers, O'Donnell.

But poor Dutton was to be hanged by Binns at Kirkdale. The latter had hanged a man for the first time just a few weeks before (Henry Powell at Wandsworth), but Dutton was only the second in line for the tyro executioner.

There was a special element of drama in the case, as two local journalists were to be present, and also Dutton had asked the chaplain to give the optional Condemned Sermon on the Sunday before the fatal hour. The sermon was given, covering three warnings that are surely totally irrelevant, if not insulting, to a condemned man: not to be drunk, not to allow a bad temper to possess you, and not to marry in haste. Unless these were likely to happen in the next world, the whole affair appears to be cruelly ironic. But in the very early hours of his last day on earth, Dutton had something to eat (cocoa, bread and butter) and took sacrament in the prison chapel.

At 7 a.m. Binns arrived. For some odd reason, the governor would not allow Binns's assistant to enter Kirkdale. It was normal practice to have a hangman together with his assistant. But the prison bell began to toll at 7.45 a.m. and, in haste, Dutton was brought to meet Binns and to be pinioned ready for the drop. Then, as the chaplain read a text relating to man's sins, the ritual walk to the scaffold began.

This final walk was in line with regulations: the chief warder led the way, followed by Dutton and two warders; then Binns was behind them, followed in line by a doctor, the under-sheriff and chaplain. So far so good. But then they reached the scaffold.

The drama came when Dutton was given the rapid final pinioning and strapping ready for the lever to be pulled; the clock had not struck 8 a.m., and Binns walked to look at his victim, causing a rather nervous atmosphere. Dutton asked Lord Jesus to receive his soul. Then the clock struck, and the lever was pulled; Dutton dropped, but it was not a quick death.

The doctor looked down at the struggling man on the rope and said, 'This is poor work, he is not dead yet.' In a drop of almost 7 feet 6 inches, the body spun and the man did not die for eight minutes. That was outrageously cruel by any standards. The doctor could see what the problem was: a very thick rope had been used (like a ship's hawser, the doctor said) and Dutton was very short, only 5 feet 2 inches. The result was what every hangman feared: slow strangulation rather than a snapping of the spinal column with speed, and the humane intention of a quick death.

There was an inquest after this farce. Mr Barker was the county coroner. The prison governor, Major Leggett, made a long statement outlining the time taken for the culprit to die, and also added that nothing had been done to 'hasten the end' of the unfortunate Dutton. The doctor's evidence would make difficult reading for anyone concerned about the terrible suffering the man had experienced: only a slight separation of two bones in the vertebrae near the point of contact with the rope had happened, rather than a sharp break. In the doctor's opinion, the noose had been placed at the wrong position near the nape of the neck, rather than under the jaw or the ear. There was, it was stated, a difference of 300 pounds in weight in the drop/body ratio.

The question that must have been on everyone's lips was boldly asked by the coroner: 'Was the executioner sober?'

Major Leggett answered that he was not sure. Then this interchange took place: something that must have ensured Binns's departure from his post:

Coroner: Has the hangman left the prison?
Leggett: Yes.
Coroner: I wish he were here.

A juryman asked the governor's opinion of the affair. Leggett said, 'I think it was inefficiently performed – clumsily. I did not like his manner of conducting the execution. He seemed, in adjusting the strap on the man, to do it in a very bungling way, which I did not like at all.'

Against the popular image of judges handing out death sentences by the dozen every day, and the busy traffic of carts with condemned felons being taken from prison to Tyburn (situated close to Marble Arch), a large proportion of those condemned were reprieved. Between 1814 and 1834 there were over 23,000 people sentenced to die, and of these only 1,518 actually were hanged on the scaffold. Many were transported and 'proclaimed' – that is, were sent into the army to fight Napoleon or work in the distant colonies. But there were times when the hangman was busy, and times when he had to hang women and children. One of the most emotive and divisive areas of criminality up until the early twentieth century was infanticide.

At York in 1800, Mary Thorp, just twenty-two years old, pleaded not guilty to a charge of 'murdering her male infant'. It was the first capital offence tried in Yorkshire in the new century. One of the very first accounts of the case, published in 1831, is restrained and keeps back much of the material around the story, simply pointing out that Mary began domestic service at fourteen, was happy, and then was seduced 'by one, whilst he pretended to lead the confiding girl on to happiness, brought her to ruin, misery and disgrace'. It appears from the records that there was no knowledge of the identity of this man.

That course of seduction and ruin is arguably the typology of the infanticide chronicle throughout centuries of English history. In Mary Thorp's case the events were chillingly simple: a woman friend helped in the birth of the child, and then, according to one reporter, a week later Mary took the child to a pond and threw it into the water, a stone tied around its neck. This appears to be too vague an account; she in fact stayed with a widow called Hartley in Sheffield, for the delivery, then said she was moving on to Derby to be with her sister. But her plan was to go to Ecclesfield. It was there, in the river near Bridge Houses, that the child was thrown to its death, with tape tied tightly around its neck.

The child had been strangled before it was thrown into the water, and there was no doubt that the tape around its neck was Mary's: Hartley identified the material. There was an inquest following this discovery of course; the charge was murder, and the coroner arranged for Mary Thorp to stand trial at York. The opinion of a commentator at the time was simple but powerful: 'The wretched girl became a miserable mother, and gave birth to a child whose smiles became her reproach.'

The defence was that the woman was not aware of what she was doing and was delirious. The medical men agreed that she had indeed suffered from 'milk fever', but that this was not sufficient cause of any palpable insanity in Mary. She had apparently intended to do the deed, and did so with awareness of the act. In spite of the fact that she did not look like a ragged victim of street poverty and likely immorality, the jury was not sympathetic, and took into consideration the circumstantial evidence, along with the point about no real insanity in Mary, and so reached a verdict of guilty.

When the sentence was passed, as reported by Thomas Rede Leman, Mary 'bore it with great firmness and curtseyed very lowly to the court before she left it'. At the York Tyburn on 17 March, she was hanged.

According to the first full report, the morality fixed as part of the judgement on Mary was entirely in keeping with the limited understanding of infanticide at the time: 'In a case like this, there can be no medium between pity for the offender, or utter abhorrence' yet the writer goes on to tackle the subject of her possible temporary insanity: 'Medical experience tells us that fevers of all descriptions affect the sanity of the sufferer: milk fever is most powerful in its effects; and though the law might condemn, society may pity such a criminal.'

It is a sad story indeed; Mary in court was a 'pale and care-worn creature' and, of course, she had been the subject of a heartless seduction. This pattern of behaviour, leading to child murder, was to preoccupy the best minds of the later Victorian period; Elizabeth Gaskell wrote her novel *Ruth* in 1853 to deal with the difficult subject of the seduction of a poor working girl by a rich man. She lost friends over this publication.

In cases like that of Mary Thorp, then, the commentaries show a great deal of sympathy, and writers were clearly aware of the clash between criminal law and moral opinion. But all this was of no use to the condemned young woman, destined to die on the scaffold. We have to admire her resolve and self-control: when the verdict was given, she stood firm, and it was noted that 'in person she was extremely prepossessing'. It has to be said, with a more modern understanding of the dynamics of a courtroom, that she should have been less prepossessing and more frail and demure. It might have had some influence on those in judgement.

As mentioned in the Introduction, there was also the horrendous issue of petty treason and its contrast with murder. Until it was abolished in 1790, there was a statute that included the act of death by burning for a wife who murdered a husband or for a servant who murdered his or her master. If a husband killed his wife, the sentence was that he should be hanged; if a wife killed a husband, then she would be burned.

The story of Elizabeth Broadingham is one of the most prominent examples of this. The narrative vaguely echoes the actions of Lady Macbeth (lacking the 'milk of human kindness') except that the setting and the motives are the lowest and most despicable imaginable.

John Broadingham, her husband, was not exactly a pillar of the community. He was locked away in York dungeons for robbery when Elizabeth began her affair with Thomas Aikney, a man younger than her. It was a case of extreme passion, 'while the cat's away', and she liked the pleasures of loving and sex with the other man so much that she moved in with him.

A man coming out of prison after all kinds of deprivations

expects some comfort and loyalty from his family. John Broadingham found none of this: he merely found that his wife had left the marital home. Elizabeth appears to have wanted more than simply living with Aikney as his partner; she wanted to be free of the marriage with John, and to remove the husband from the scene altogether was her aim.

She began to work on Aikney with a view to leading him into murdering John. The younger man at first resisted these pleas and wiles, but after some time he began to be influenced. It is recounted, though not definitely known, that Elizabeth made sure that Aikney had plenty of alcohol in him and tempted him in all the ways she could invent, as she allured him into a murderous pact. He finally went along with the plan.

Elizabeth must have been a very influential speaker and something of an actress; not only had she inveigled her way into Aikney's life, she now played the part of good wife, returning to John and apparently wanting to return to the marital harmony they once had. John took her back. But only a week or so after moving back home, she was talking to Thomas Aikney about their plan, and sorting out the details of where and when it would be done. The lover still vainly tried to resist, but she was relentless. Poor Thomas thought that the best move was to run away and avoid the confrontation, to make a new start elsewhere.

Things came to a head on the night of 8 February 1776 when Elizabeth woke her husband as there was a loud noise downstairs; John staggered down to investigate and made his way to the door where Aikney was pounding on the wood. As John Broadingham opened up, Aikney knifed him in the chest and then, as the frenzied attack continued, he stabbed the man in the thigh and the leg. With the knife stuck in his belly, John managed to walk out into the street where he was seen by neighbours.

So badly was the husband hurt that he had almost been eviscerated in the assault; he was clutching his stomach and his guts were exposed. The report at the time states that he was 'supporting his bowels'.

John Broadingham died the day after the attack. It took only a short time for neighbours and the magistrate to find Aikney and then the whole story was revealed. Elizabeth and Thomas confessed and Aikney was hanged at York on 20 March 1776. In this tale lies the incredible difference between punishment for murder and petty treason; Aikney's body, as was the custom, was cut down and then transported to Leeds Infirmary for use in dissection work with medical education. But Elizabeth had committed petty treason. Her fate was to be burnt at the stake. The only humane act in these cases was that the executioner normally strangled the woman before the fire was set alight, and he did so for Elizabeth. She was burnt and some ghoulish witnesses collected her ashes as souvenirs.

Mercy never entered into the matter when a woman was considered for the death penalty in the late eighteenth century and in the early nineteenth century. The great journalist of the period, J. W. Robertson Scott, has a memory of a woman on a scaffold at this time: '…it was an old woman, a mere old wrinkled, wretched bundle. She was said to have killed a bastard. She cried, "You cannot hang me!" But they did.'

As noted, there were pardons, respites and reprieves. Until the eighteenth century, these had been primarily given by the sovereign. When there was such a person as the Home Secretary, things changed.

The Home Office was formed in 1782 after radical parliamentary structural changes. There had been two departments of state for hundreds of years, one for the Northern Department (dealing with Europe) and one for the Southern Department (dealing with France and the colonies). These were both foreign offices, of course. The secretary handling affairs at home was of no real consequence; but then Charles James Fox began the move to create what became the Home Office, a responsibility for home and colonial business.

In terms of law and the criminal justice system, for centuries the structure had been that each county had a Lord Lieutenant and a sheriff, with the magistrates acting with them. For instance, these persons were present at a hanging: the specific order of the ritual walk to the scaffold involved the Lord Lieutenant and sheriff as well as the prisoner governor, the priest, doctor and hangman. But from 1782 there would be a Home Secretary and he would be the person at the head of the criminal justice system. The Earl of Shelburne became the first man to take that post.

The Recorder's Report came from what became known as the 'Hanging Cabinet'. Various dignitaries would sit and deliberate on the fate of the listed felons from the assize recommendations. The report would then go to the Privy Council and from there matters would reach the executive stage and things would happen. There were mistakes: in 1833 there was a list of respited prisoners sent in the report, and there was just one name omitted from the pardons: Job Cox, who had stolen £5 from a letter. The names were printed in the

COURTESY OF H.M.S.O.

The Recorder making his report. At this meeting, the fates of those convicted of capital crimes at the assizes were decided.

national newspapers, and there was the name of Job Cox, who was to hang. He was awaiting his fate in Newgate prison when Sir Thomas Denman, the Lord Chief Justice of the King's Bench, saw the list of names; he thought it was simply an error caused by a press reporter working too hastily, and luckily for the condemned man, Denman mentioned this to the under-sheriff, who said that the list was right and that the authorities at Newgate had been told to prepare the man for the scaffold. *The Times* reported the exciting and dramatic consequences of that conversation between lawyers:

> 'What!' said Sir Thomas Denman, 'Cox ordered for execution… Impossible! I was myself one of the Privy Council when the report was made, and I know that no warrant for the execution of anyone was issued. Cox was ordered to be placed in solitary confinement and to be kept to hard labour, previously to his being transported for life, to which punishment the judgement to die was commuted.' The under sheriff was very glad to be the bearer of good tidings at Newgate…

The reporter explained for the public the nature of the Recorder's Report: 'It does not consist of a transcript of the shorthand-writer's notes of every particular case, but is merely the condensed account of each case made by the Recorder himself from the shorthand-writer's notes. It is of course liable to some objection…' That was the understatement of the year for poor Cox.

The Recorder's Report was a matter of great public interest; in 1820, while the king was at Brighton and there had been a high-profile trial of a murder of a gamekeeper at York, clearly the newspapers had to tell the readers who followed the trial that the fate of the killer was in the hands of the Hanging Cabinet. *The Times* reported simply that, 'The King is expected from Brighton tomorrow to receive the Recorder's report.'

When we think of prisons and their death cells and scaffolds, though, the Victorian and Edwardian periods define much of our general popular cultural attitudes and knowledge. This is because the advancement of newspapers and popular periodicals had multiplied then, and the beginnings of mass media meant that the general public could follow the progress of the prisoner from trial to cell and to the hangman with intense detail and a generous element of vicarious excitement and fear. This was very much the case with some major Victorian criminals, and representative of this is Palmer the poisoner.

Palmer poisoned fourteen people, all in order to gather some cash to feed his gambling habit. The gambling was unsuccessful and the debts mounted; although he was a fairly successful physician in Rugeley, setting up his practice in 1846, he had a wild streak which included fathering several illegitimate children and following slow horses at the courses. Murder was the simplest way out of his problems, he thought, and so he began to use his knowledge of drugs and poisons to see off all kinds of people.

His first victim was his mother-in-law, who had come to live with his family in 1848; she died soon after arriving and her possessions and cash went to Mrs Palmer – which meant effectively that Palmer had the money to spend of course. By 1854, deaths in the Palmer household were more frequent than the average – even in that time when infant mortality was high. By that particular year, four children and an uncle had died in the house; when his wife died, Palmer was left a very large sum of money, and the income from insurance firms was considerable. But the gambling continued, and after the doctor's brother died, the insurance people became suspicious and refused to pay out yet again.

What eventually caught him out was the death of his gambling friend, John Cook. They had both had a day out at Shrewsbury races and when they came home they went for drinks, as Cook had made some money (Palmer had lost as usual). But when Cook was ill at the party, and was subsequently treated by Palmer before he died, the suspicions around the doctor's circle were too positive and rabid to ignore. The law paid him a visit and he was charged with murder. He had to be tried in London, such was the local hatred. In May 1856 he stood in the dock at the Old Bailey. It was a most notorious case. *The Daily Telegraph* reported on 27 May:

> Each day since Palmer was first arraigned at the bar of the Old Bailey, among all classes of society, from the ennobled peer down to the most

humble of London costermongers, there has been one grand prevailing desire to hear the trial, and if possible, to obtain a glimpse of the Rugeley hero of poisoning notoriety. Every morning has attracted crowds of spectators to the vicinity…from Ludgate Hill to Newgate prison there was a dense crowd of people prior to the opening of the court…

When Palmer was sentenced and the prospect of such a celebrity villain being hanged was appreciated, the fervour was uncontainable in the media. The public had also learned a good deal about the nature of strychnine, Palmer's chosen poison. Letters to *The Times* and other papers educated the readers on this, on several occasions. One writer noted that:

In proof of the correctness of the pinion that strychnine remains in the bodies of animals killed by it, permit me to quote a single instance…On a fox being found dead and the proprietor of the covert being blamed for it, on enquiry it appeared that some hens' eggs had been contaminated with strychnine, that a rook and magpie had eaten these…and then been eaten by the fox…

On Saturday 14 June at 8 a.m. Throttler Smith executed Palmer at Stafford. Barriers had been placed in the main road and in the street where the scaffold was erected. As well as 150 of the regular police force of the county, a large number of special constables was assembled. The authorities were well aware that a huge crowd would gather. *The Daily Telegraph* set the scene:

The inns of Stafford drove a busy trade on Friday. All day long, people flocked into the town, by road, by rail, on foot, on horseback, in gig, carriage or on donkey. Such crowding at the railway station, such jostling in the tavern yards, tavern parlours and coffee rooms, such crowding and pushing in public houses…Beds had been at a premium for days before, for everybody wanted to get shelter…There was no bed to be got, not for love nor money…

People with an eye to business had provided stands that would be good viewing points for the hanging; costs for these ranged from five shillings to a guinea. Primitive Methodists arrived to walk with banners proclaiming 'Prepare to Meet Thy God' and walked around with papers warning of the dangers of gambling.

The press took a deep interest in the condemned man's last week in the prison, noting all visitors; Palmer's brothers and sister went to see him, and he would not see his one remaining son. The press commented: 'The poor child, it appears, is still at Rugeley with his grandmother; he has been informed that his father has gone to some distant part of the country and is anxious for his return...' The chaplain was with Palmer most of the night, and readers were told that Palmer had a cup of tea but nothing to eat, and that he was prepared for the ordeal.

The other element in prison life that has always related to the possibility of escaping the noose or other extreme penalty of the law is the appeal. There was no separate, dedicated Court of Criminal Appeal until 1907. To read accounts of appeal cases now from the early twentieth century is to confront the high drama of a hearing that was often a matter of life or death. The condemned sat and watched, listened and no doubt prayed, as legal arguments among the professional barristers progressed, and the outcome of it all could mean that the convict either walked back to prison, walked free, or walked to the noose.

On a summer day in 1908, the city of Bradford was shocked by the breaking news of a brutal murder, and it was most disturbing as it had happened in the afternoon. Thomas Wilkinson, working at Fieldhouse and Jowett in Swain Street, was beaten to death by someone wielding a poker, and the killer had brought the weapon with him, as there was no coal fire in the store.

The murderer was not exactly careful to cover his tracks or to hide his identity in any way; not only had he been seen standing in the doorway by a passer-by, looking troubled, and actually saying that, 'They were having a bit of bother in the office', but he also bought the poker just down the road, as Samuel Ellis, who sold him the weapon, was to testify.

From these details, it would appear that there may not have been a motive, as it was the nasty work of someone who was distracted in the extreme, but there was in fact a clear motive. The killer was John Ellwood, and he had worked for Fieldhouse and Jowett, leaving that employment about six months before this incident. He had been involved in a heated row with his employers and had left under a cloud; it was therefore not hard for the police to show that, as an employee, he would know the routine of the place in a typical week, and would therefore be aware that large amounts of money were brought to the building by the company cashier every Friday. It was no coincidence, perhaps, that Ellwood had arranged to visit the premises at 2 p.m. on Friday, 31 July. There had been correspondence, and both Ellwood and Wilkinson had written or rung up to leave messages. There was also the testimony of the landlord of the Fountain Brewery, who had seen the accused leave his pub just before the time of the killing.

It was hardly going to be a problem for the investigating officers, as there was plenty of blood on Ellwood's clothes when he was arrested, and his pathetic excuse that the cause of this was merely a bleeding nose was not going to fool anyone. His line of thought regarding his reasons for being seen at the murder scene that day by the man going by (he was Isaac Pollard) was simply that Wilkinson was trying to have him reinstated in his post; Mrs Ellwood produced evidence of a letter from Wilkinson to that effect, and also stated that her husband had been with her at home at the time of the murder.

All fairly straightforward, we might think. When Ellwood appeared at Leeds assizes on 12 November that year, it was revealed that his intention was to have a wages cheque, intended for the employees of the mills, to be cashed. Ellwood, it was claimed, was planning to rob Wilkinson of that cash. Later, at appeal, it was stated that a witness who had been bound over to attend the trial had not actually been called, and the lawyers at the time argued that this evidence would not have been helpful for the defence case.

At the Court of Appeal on 20 November, Mr Gregory Ellis, for the applicant Ellwood, argued that at the trial there was no motive for the murder defined and explained. The supposed letter from

Wilkinson inviting him to come regarding a job had been dismissed, but Ellwood's defence brought this up again. Mr Justice Channel explained the situation, as Ellwood stood and wondered if he was to be saved from the noose, that, '...there is a great deal of difference between absence of proved motive and proved absence of motive'. In other words, that the accused planned to go to the premises and steal, and to steal even at the cost of a life, appeared to be the motive, and no letter arranging a meeting would cast doubt on that. After all, he had been seen by a man at the time, and it was known that he had bought the poker. There was no ambiguity in the material evidence of the nature of the killing: the victim was battered brutally and relentlessly, the wounds inflicted by the poker.

The appeal was refused. John Ellwood became another client of executioner Henry Pierrepoint, and he was hanged on 3 December 1908 at Armley gaol.

There was also, in earlier times, before the press expanded in the later nineteenth century, the phenomenon of the 'ordinary's narrative'. The ordinary of the prison (usually Newgate, but other prisons followed suit) took down a biography from the lips of the man during his stay in the condemned cell, and this was often combined into a 'last dying speech' which was sold on the streets. The artist Thomas Rowlandson depicted a woman selling these speeches, showing how popular they were. Both the speeches and the broadsheet biographies sold well and made printers wealthy. Later, hangmen's memoirs became very popular, and their stories opened up the reality of how prison staff coped when the condemned did everything to avoid their deaths, fighting or struggling all the way to the noose, as was the case with Mary Lefley, as we know from her hangman's autobiography.

James Berry, the executioner, was aware that William Lefley, her husband and victim, was something of a simpleton and 'mentally challenged'; he worked as a carrier, and his approach to business made him some enemies as well as men who would ridicule him. He made a few enemies in this respect. There were factors about this that never came up at Mary's trial, and Berry, new to the job and keen to do things right, was thinking he was about to hang an innocent woman.

But he was a professional, with a task ahead of him and he carried on. He wrote his own account of the process in his memoirs:

> To the very last she protested her innocence, though the night before she was very restless and constantly exclaimed, 'Lord, Thou knowest all!' She would have no breakfast and when I approached her she was in a nervous agitated state, praying to God for salvation...but as an innocent woman...she had to be led to the scaffold by two female warders.

Berry records that Mary, when he went to fetch her on the fateful morning, was ill. She also shouted 'Murder!' Berry wrote with feeling and some repugnance about the whole business, right to the point of

SECRETS OF THE PRISON HOUSE, 1880

The execution suite at Lincoln. This clearly shows the two levels, the condemned cell being above the area where the body would fall with the coffin waiting. Felons hanged were usually buried within the prison grounds.

having to pinion her. He noted that her cries as she was dragged along to the scaffold were piercing. As Berry reported, 'Our eyes were downcast, our sense numbed, and down the cheeks of some the tears were rolling.' After all, as soon as Berry arrived at the prison, a woman warder had said to him, 'She has never ceased to protest her innocence. Oh Mr Berry, I am sure as can be that she never committed that dreadful crime. You have only to talk to the woman to know that…' Berry noted, as he arrived, that he 'found the prison in a state of panic'. He recalled that on the fateful morning, the chaplain's prayers had sounded 'more like a sob'.

The years between c.1850 and 1900 were a great age of documentary enquiry, and writers and journalists, artists and photographers took a deep interest in all aspects of what was referred to as 'the criminal classes'. Prison and prisoners were clearly a part of this interest. Prison visitors were common, and the movement for reform, emerging from Evangelical Christianity and other related charitable organizations, was a powerful force for social change. Also in these years, the police force was considerably accelerated into modern thinking, having to cope with new types of prisoners such as anarchists and bombers. A prominent example of this was the execution of Fenians and other assassins, and perhaps the most sensational of the assassinations by Irish nationalists was the Phoenix Park murder.

William Marwood, the Lincolnshire hangman, went to Ireland to hang the assassins. This gang had murdered the Chief Secretary for Ireland, Lord Frederick Cavendish, and his Under-Secretary, in broad daylight in Phoenix Park, Dublin, while the victims were walking in the park. Four men had leapt from a cab and stabbed them to death. The 'Irish Invincibles', as they called themselves, sent black-bordered cards to the Dublin papers. Joseph Brady had gone with one group and Daniel Curley with another, after a planning meeting at Wrenn's Tavern near Dublin Castle. They agreed to split up and decide on where the attack should take place. They had made sure that they had correctly identified Harry Burke, the Under-Secretary, so there would be no mistakes. As they were gathering in the park, there was almost a very big problem for them because a police superintendent called Mallon was going to the park to meet one of his contacts and he met a plain-clothes detective who warned him of an attempt on his life; Mallon left, so the coast was clear for the assassins.

Another turn of fate for the victims was that Cavendish had been offered a ride instead, but had insisted that he walk with Burke. As Cavendish was only just in place as Chief Secretary, there were things to talk through, and a stroll seemed a pleasant way to do that. But they were walking to an appointment with death. After a man called Timothy Kelly had advanced and knifed Cavendish, the gang were soon upon them, with Brady cutting Burke's throat in the assault. They made their escape, hoping to drive around the city and approach Dublin from another entrance, thus making a platform for some kind of alibi, but a detective had seen a number of them and would later identify them. The first move in apprehending the gang came when a driver broke down and told the tale. It was not long before they were tried and sentenced and William Marwood was crossing the Irish Sea with his ropes and pinion.

Sixteen of the Invincibles were tried and five were hanged; James Carey turned state's evidence. Joseph Brady was executed on 14 May, sentenced to death by Mr Justice O'Brien, and others followed, with Marwood hanging them at Kilmainham prison. The events went down in popular history, as in the song 'Monto' recorded by The Dubliners, in which we have the rhyme:

> When Carey told on Skin-the-goat
> O'Donnell caught him on the boat
> He wished he'd never been afloat, the filthy skite.
> 'Twasn't very sensible
> To tell on the Invincibles
> They stood up for their principles, day and night.

However, the British government's treatment of Fenian prisoners received criticisms; there were rumours of prisoners in Mountjoy jail, Dublin, being buried alive, but this was a ridiculous myth. Between 1865 and 1868 sixty Fenian prisoners passed through Mountjoy, sentenced to penal servitude. They would be destined for English prisons eventually. Although they were classed as ordinary prisoners, they were naturally treated with a high level of security in mind as they were violent, dangerous men.

One of the prominent Fenians, O'Donovan Rossa, wrote about his journey to Mountjoy: 'The van rattled through the streets, the soldiers galloped at each side of it with sabres drawn, and in less than half an hour the world closed upon me inside the portals of Mountjoy.'

In terms of hangings, Ireland presented a problem for the prison authorities: an Irish hangman could not be found. A Yorkshireman called Scott travelled, as well as Binns and Marwood, to perform hangings in Dublin. Even later, Henry 'Harry' Pierrepoint travelled across, and was to be severely tested by one of the most bizarre executions ever done, and that was the hanging of Richard Heffernan in Dublin in 1910. The scene that was to emerge was one of tragic-comedy – but very dark comedy nevertheless.

Heffernan had killed a girl called Mary Walker, stabbing her and then telling people that he had seen the murder. But fate had a string of stressful incidents lined up for the Pierrepoints. First, something happened that illustrates the essential need for the hangman to protect the privacy of his identity. For some reason unknown at the time, Harry's name was on the passenger list of the ferry they were taking from Holyhead. People obviously began to take a vicarious and morbid pleasure in knowing who he was; the public hangman was always a figure of intense media interest. Wisely, he was given a private place in which to hide for the journey.

The next incident in the Heffernan fiasco was that the condemned had been so unbalanced and determined to flout the hangman that he had set about clawing at his own throat to take his own life. In normal practice, suicide was high on the agenda of a hanging in the planning of the official personnel involved. The man was sedated and put on close guard. The brothers were aware that this was a highly unusual and challenging case. They knew that they would not only have to be acutely aware of the need for precise attention to all safety procedures, but that the victim was likely to do the most unexpected things at any time.

There were priests in attendance and they came to speak with the brothers on the night before the hanging; no doubt there was extended discussion of Heffernan's condition. What Harry must have noticed – and it became important the next day – was that there was a very small space on the trapdoor area by the drop. What happened there the next day was that the condemned man strode into the trapdoor area with a gaggle of priests; he was weeping and praying and kissing the cross. But speed was the first consideration here, and even when Tom did his pinioning well and stood back, there were the priests, still on the trapdoor. There was no alternative: decorum must be broken, and the priests pushed hard out of the way. That's what Harry did, and then down went the lever.

Until 1964 executions continued, and they always presented special problems and challenges to the prisons. Often, the condemned aroused a great deal of public sympathy, and governors and staff had to cope with crowds and demonstrations at the prison gates. But gradually, the hanging days came to an end. Albert Pierrepoint, who had hanged hundreds of people in his long career, including Nazis after the Nuremburg trials, famously said: 'I do not now believe that any one of the hundreds of executions I carried out has in any way acted as a deterrent against future murder.'

Finally, what about the criminals who escaped the noose on the day they walked on to the scaffold? Examples are very rare. There was a man known as 'Half-hanged Smith' who served at sea on a man o' war after being apprenticed in London to a packer. After that he joined the army and was in a guards regiment, but he was always destined for a life of crime and fell into bad company.

Smith was active as a thief at a time when over two hundred capital crimes were on the statute books, so it was not difficult at that time for a villain to find himself on a journey to the scaffold at Tyburn. Smith stood against five indictments and indeed the judge put on the black cap and sentenced him to death.

To Tyburn he went, with the usual crowd gathering. The stages in the familiar ritual took place: the slow drive down Oxford Street and the arrival at the hanging tree. Then the speeches from the scaffold and the expected repentance or defiance. Smith appeared to be fond of a dying speech, but was not really openly concerned about being 'turned off' and was hanged. At that time, the art of hanging was an uncertain business and the hangmen were usually drunks and criminals doing the distasteful work to gain their own remission or even freedom.

Consequently, Smith had been dangling and fighting for life on the end of the rope for some minutes when a voice cried, 'A reprieve!' He was cut down. Fortunately, he had no close friends or family, because if he had, they would have pulled and swung on his legs to hasten his end.

Smith was asked what it felt like to be strangled by a drunk and he said, 'When I was turned off I was sensible for some time of a very great pain, as my body is weighty…I felt my spirits to be in a great commotion, and I saw a great blaze, a blinding light which seemed to go out of my eyes with a flash, then I lost all sense of pain.'

The lucky man was back to his life of crime, though, and once again before the judge and jury. But at the Old Bailey for house-breaking, there was a special verdict and he walked free. On the third trial in his life, after again robbing the good citizens of London, he would almost certainly have been to Tyburn again, except that the prosecutor died before the trial began. The commentators at the time considered it fitting that he should turn to Christ and leave off his criminal career, after such special providential care of his life. But it seems unlikely that he stopped his burglaries.

Smith was the son of a Malton farmer in North Yorkshire. His parents and relatives must have read about him, such was his short-lived fame, but none came to see him die, as far as we know, and if they had done, he would certainly have died.

However, the records in respect of fate and circumstances stepping in to prevent a hanging relates to a man called John Lee. In 2000, at an auction in Mere, Wiltshire, a noose used at Exeter prison in 1885 was sold for £3,058. The buyers were the Crime Through Time Museum at Newent in Gloucestershire. This was the noose that failed to hang John Lee. In fact, the hangman and his paraphernalia failed three times to hang the man, a footman who had killed his employer,

Emma Keyse in Babbacombe. Lee became known as John Babbacombe Lee, 'The man they could not hang'. In 1897 the mystery as
to what went wrong with the contraptions for hanging on the day he
was to hang was solved. An engineer called Cyril Penny reported
that the pit below the platform gallows was subject to flooding and
the damp had warped and rotted the trapdoor. Lee was freed from
prison on licence in 1909, but after the failed executions he had not
returned to his normal cell: the governor left him in the death cell for
a month, maybe as one last piece of mental torture after the frustra-
tion of failing to see him swing.

William Calcraft,
the public hangman,
busy between 1829
and 1868

LAURA CARTER

9

Women Prisoners

There has already been much discussion in earlier chapters of suffragettes and of infanticide – two notable peaks in the long graph of women and the criminal law throughout British history. Now a closer look is required.

Not all women in trouble with the law in times past were as fortunate as Bet Flint, acquaintance of Dr Johnson, who was in court charged with stealing a counterpane. She was lucky to have a judge who was notoriously fond of 'a good wench' – the controversial Lord Chief Justice Willes. Bet was acquitted and is on record as saying, afterwards, 'Now that the counterpane is my own, I shall make a petticoat out of it!' For most women in her time, the 1750s, a theft of that nature could easily have meant a spell in Newgate with the smelly and disease-ridden underclass of Georgian London.

In one of the most influential tracts on English law, the great legal writer and lawyer Sir William Blackstone wrote in his master work, *Commentaries on the Laws of England*, 'The husband and wife are one person in law; that is, the very being or legal existence of the woman is suspended during her marriage, or at least is incorporated or consolidated into that of her husband...' Reading accounts of women offenders over the centuries, it is easy to see how this condition of being a mere 'chattel' had horrendous consequences. Blackstone's book was published in 1769, but if we go back to the earliest laws –

those of the Anglo-Saxons – we see the source of inequality and the nature of women as possessions.

Before any national criminal justice system there were kings in various parts of the Anglo-Saxon areas and they made their own codes of law. At that time, crimes committed were put right by payments to the victims: damage to an eye cost fifty shillings, and to a toenail just sixpence. Adultery and fornication were expensive hobbies – the Church had a say in these matters of course. Through the Middle Ages, women as victims were in a tough position. The court rolls of Lincolnshire, for instance, in the twelfth century, show that savage attacks and rapes committed at night on lonely households were often punished merely with fines. Even in the great Magna Carta of 1215, they could not accuse anyone of a murder except in the case of a woman's husband being killed.

But as criminals, women generally appeared at the quarter sessions for their locality for offences relating to desperation and poverty. When they stood in the dock for serious crime, at assizes usually, that was a rare occurrence compared to men, and the crimes were generally linked to sex, motherhood or what we would now think of as 'crimes of passion'.

If we look at the everyday quarter sessions reports from the Elizabethan period to the nineteenth century, we find sad instances of women involved in crime. In a hearing for Doncaster for instance, we have much robbery, theft, and breaking and entering going on, but women are not often part of these gangs – they acted alone: a widow called Katherine Booth broke into a house and stole a chest of goods, and Margaret Chambers stole a waistcoat, a petticoat and 'a pecke of oatemeale'. Petty theft was going on all the time, and it was often opportunistic, as with two women of Brampton Byerley, who stole twelve sheaves of barley.

For women as for men, the 'benefit of clergy' ruling applied (see page 28); if this was allowed, women were branded in court.

When it came to witchcraft, it was a punishable offence from very early times, but the most celebrated cases were in 'epidemic' instances such as in the Elizabethan and Jacobean times, and again in the 1640s. By the end of the seventeenth century, attitudes changed, and the last execution in England was that of Alice Molland in 1684. The Witchcraft Act of 1736 made prosecutions for the offence illegal.

As mentioned in Chapter 8, through the centuries, infanticide emerges as the one specifically female offence. It was a crime that only a mother could commit, and by a statute of 1624 the offender was defined as an unmarried mother. Court records (and execution records too) show a large number of sentences and hangings for this offence, though increasingly courts took a more lenient view. In 1803 an Act was passed that made it essential for the prosecution to prove that the death was intended by the mother, not caused by natural illness. But it was not until the Infanticide Act of 1938 that it was set apart from murder, taking into account the concept of postnatal depression. The phrasing was that mothers who may have taken the infant's life were 'disturbed by reason of not having fully recovered from the effects of giving birth'.

Of course, abortion was linked to this, and that was not legalized until 1967; in the Edwardian and late Victorian years, with cases of baby-farming and back-street abortion, capital sentences were common. The related crime of 'concealing a birth' by a young mother was also very common throughout the Victorian period, and sentences could be severe, although more enlightened thought created reformatories and other institutions rather than prisons for these female offenders.

'The oldest profession' was often the province of the church courts – the so-called 'bawdy courts' which would have dealt with local cases. But this has always been very hard to regulate. In a publication on crime in London published in 1795, Patrick Colquhoun stated that there were 50,000 women in prostitution. For the Victorians, it became a problem needing attention when the health of the Empire's soldiers and sailors was at risk. The Contagious Diseases Acts of the 1860s made it possible to report a woman suspected of prostitution if she was working within ten miles of certain garrison towns. She had to report to a magistrate and then go to a hospital to be 'inspected'.

One of the most horrendous punishments a woman could suffer until the 1790s was burning at the stake – but this was not for witch-craft, but for petty treason. Until that time, if a man killed his wife,

he had committed murder, but if a wife murdered her husband, the crime was petty treason (as opposed to high treason – against the state), and though he would be hanged, she would be burned. As mentioned earlier, common practice was for the executioner to be given money to strangle the poor victim before the fire was lit.

Of course, for the more everyday, usually relationship-related killing, convictions of women were few. After the 1860s executions for murder were less frequent and capital crimes were reduced to just four. Between 1868 (when public hangings were abolished) and 1955, there were forty hangings of women, the last being Ruth Ellis. To illustrate the figures for men and women hanged: in the twentieth century there was a total of 865 executions, and of these only 18 were women.

On the whole, the history of women in the criminal law in Britain has been related to the national, fundamental struggle for rights such as the vote and for equality within marriage and in careers. Yet, it is astonishing that prison is still the standard punishment for women. In a report led by Baroness Corston in 2006, the conclusion was that most women who commit a crime should be dealt with in the community, and that a network of women's centres for these offenders be set up. The controversy continues with regard to women's relationship to crime – whether the offence is 'business' crime or an offence done in desperation – so in a sense nothing fundamental has changed.

With all this in mind, what was life in prison like for female offenders? Very large numbers were transported, many from 1786 to Australia and, before the loss of the American colonies, to the British settlements on the Eastern seaboard of the United States. Women convicted of a child murder in Long Riston, Yorkshire, in 1799 would have been pilloried, sent to York Castle, and then put on board a hulk (a prison ship) in the Thames estuary before sailing for Australia. The first fleet to Botany Bay left in 1786 and transportation continued until 1868. The women on these ships had a very

Opposite: The burning of a woman. This illustrates the severe and barbaric penalty for the crime of petty treason, in this case the murder of a husband by a wife.

hard time, of course. When the very first fleet left England there were eleven ships and there were 586 males and 191 females on board. As historians have shown, the women were hard to control and prostitution was rife. Sometimes the women were put in irons for this practice, as aboard the *Lady Penrhyn* in 1787.

A typical case would be like that of Charlotte Barnacle, who was convicted of murder, along with her friend. They had put arsenic in the tea of their employer, not intending to kill her but to make her suffer a little. Clearly they did something that was very wrong. But the jury were lenient, and although the judge was sure that they had intended a malicious act, it was agreed that they were not guilty of 'intending to take away life'.

Charlotte arrived in Hobart in 1843, and there she married and had a child. But she and her husband absconded and began a new life in mainland Australia, where they were involved in the mining industry in Tarrawingee. She died in 1896, aged seventy-three.

On the journey, Charlotte would have worn clothes of flannel. In 1849, Alexander Kilroy was campaigning for women convicts to be given thicker and stronger shoes, because he reckoned their thin old shoes were a cause of catarrhal illness. There was no clothing

The *Discovery* hulk. This is pictured at Deptford in 1829. Decommissioned ships were used to hold prisoners, mostly during the period *c.* 1830.

MAYHEW AND BINNY, *THE CONVICT PRISONS OF LONDON*

available for the children who came on board; they were in rags from start to finish. Later, the Quaker Elizabeth Fry had an impact on conditions for women on the ships; she formed ladies' committees and this meant that each individual made a parcel of gifts to give to each female convict before her ship left port. This parcel contained a hessian apron and a black cloth one, with a cotton cap and a hessian bag; by 1842, women were being given white jackets and checkered aprons in their rations.

Provisions were not so bad. Female prisoners had tea and sugar, and later there was preserved meat and potatoes. But the quantities were not great; in 1844 a man called Clarke was trying to increase the ration of one pound of meat for the whole voyage. But there were four sit-down meals a week on some ships, and the fare included pork plum pudding and gruel.

Deaths on the voyages were still high. On six ships sailing between 1792 and 1794, 5 women out of 200 died. One problem was the status and nature of the naval surgeon. As Charles Bateson has written:

> As with the naval agent, no attempt was made to define the naval surgeon's powers or to invest him with the requisite authority...His lowly position increased his difficulties with the commissioned officers in command of the guard and with masters.

Their journals often give us insights into what women had to endure, as in this instance of a punishment: 'In all the course of my life I never heard such expressions come from the mouth of a human being. The woman's hands were tied behind her back and she was gagged.' The woman in question, Elizabeth Barber, had her hands tied behind her back and was gagged, and she was left like that through the night. Several women were ironed on this particular trip. The journal says, 'The damned whores the moment that they got below, fell a fighting amongst one another.'

But aboard a ship called the *Friendship* it was very different. There, the women did the washing and mending for the officers. One officer noted that they were perfectly behaved for the whole voyage.

Generally, if the felon's destination was a convict ship, then they had escaped the noose and, if they could survive the journey, they would have a chance of a decent new life. They were often given a ticket of leave after five years of good behaviour, which meant that they could go into domestic service or farm work outside the prison colony.

What about the woman who had killed but who was classified as insane? In the years up to the mid-nineteenth century, the asylums could be horrendous, as the basic treatment was forcible restraint and violent suppression of any behaviour deemed unacceptable. Of course, if a person was 'criminally insane' then there was the added perspective of staff not seeing any value in showing them kindness or consideration. It was as late as 1808 that there was any legislation allowing public funds to go into asylums, and it was in 1845 that provision of county asylums was made mandatory.

In York there was a scandal in 1813 after a public inquiry into the asylum there. Yorkshire women who had killed ended up in that asylum when they escaped the scaffold, and their time there was not good at all. The management were dismissed in that year and new staff were brought in. Luckily for York, the new manager was Dr

FROM AN ENGRAVING BY T.H. SHEPHERD, c.1828

One of the newer asylums for the care of the insane. As legislation was gradually created to offer alternatives to prison, institutions such as this were established.

Matthew Allen, the doctor who was later to find fame as the physician who cared for the poet John Clare at High Beech in Epping. Allen was a Yorkshireman and had wandered a little before taking this post, but there, he qualified as a doctor and made the place more humane and open-minded in attitudes.

Asylums were regulated by local boards and there was a system of licensing and of inspection as the Victorian period wore on. A murderer sent to a Yorkshire asylum would have still been restrained, but there would be hot and cold baths and supervision. There were, of course, abuses in the early years, with some asylums using whips on patients. But they could also be very humane places and aware of such things as self-harm and suicide risk. For the general public, an asylum still meant 'Bedlam' with all that represented. Public asylums could be very large, as in Colney Hatch in London, a place with over 3,000 patients. For some, the tendency in the nineteenth century was for county and borough asylums to become merely custodial institutions, and arguably this was caused by the legislation of 1874 which transferred some of the costs of running the asylums to central funding.

In spite of the rise of psychiatry and the emergence of professional

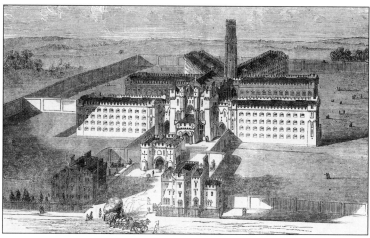

MAYHEW AND BINNY, *THE CONVICT PRISONS OF LONDON*

Holloway: the new city prison. It first opened in 1851 for men and women, but from 1903 it was for women only.

medical staff who specialized in mental health care, even in the early to mid-twentieth century a case in court in which a murder trial hinged on a defence of insanity often caused major problems.

Apart from transportation and asylums (the latter for the 'criminally insane'), women mixed with men in the local prisons, as noted in Chapters 2 and 4. Despite the recommendations from boards of enquiry, until Holloway was established as all-female in 1903, mixed prison populations had continued.

Holloway had been built and opened in 1852, but was mixed. In Lincoln prison, it was around the same time, 1902, that women were moved from there to Nottingham. Babies were born inside prison walls, of course, and in debtors' prisons, in earlier times, families would be existing in a 'normal' domestic setting as much as possible, as long as funds could be obtained.

Women in the years before the nineteenth century were committed for bastardy, and John Howard commented on this during a visit to Derbyshire county bridewell in 1776: 'A court is now made from one of the keeper's gardens, and there is a cellar for the women…in which I saw a sad object committed for bastardy.' When he visited the obnoxious Fleet prison, he was appalled to see the great numbers of women and children crammed into both the 'Master's Side' for those able to pay fees and the 'Common Side' – for the desperate cases: 'Seeing the prison crowded with women and children, I procured an accurate list of them and for that on 6 April, 1776 there were on the Master's side 213 prisoners and on the Common side 30…their wives and children were 475.'

Of course, serious crimes involving women offenders, ranging from witchcraft to murder and infanticide, provide a range of destinations within the criminal justice system of the time. Sometimes there is a simple, plain entry in a calendar of prisoners, as this at Canterbury in 1640: 'Alice Howland: She is attainted for murthering her bastard child and she is to be hanged until dead.' Witchcraft usually demanded longer explanations, as in the case of Hanna Baker at the West Kent quarter sessions in 1704:

Convicted for witchcraft and inchanting of cattell, must remaine in prison for the space of one whole year next ensuing without bail or mainprise* and must stand four times openly upon the pillory in the town and village of Eleham in this county by the space of six hours every time, viz: the first market that happens there after Ladyday, Midsummer, Michaelmas and Christmas next and openly confess her offence. [*A mainprise was a sheriff's writ to bind an offender to appear at a certain time.]

In cases of witchcraft the women were caught in exercises of male authority and power, as the story of the famous Lancashire witches makes clear. This is a case that smacks of corruption and skulduggery. Some historians have argued that Jennet Preston from Gisburn was hanged because she was the mistress of one Thomas Lister and, in being that woman, was hated by Lister's son. Before her fatal trial that led to her death sentence, Jennet had been acquitted during the famous period of the 'Lancashire Witches' who had been tried at Lancaster. But after coming through that phase of crazed and irrational prosecution, she stood in the dock again in July 1612, accused of the murder of Thomas Lister.

Recent research on the case makes it clear that two powerful men, Roger Nowell (who had been high sheriff of Lancashire) and Thomas Lister of Arnoldsbiggin, which was a manor house in Gisburn, Yorkshire, perceived witchcraft as a devilish, evil concept, not as something linked to the old ideas of the 'wise woman' who was a combination of quack healer and astronomer in many communities through Britain for centuries. We have an account of the Lister–Preston story in a publication of 1613 called *The Arraignement and Trial of Jennet Preston of Gisborne in Craven in the County of York* by Thomas Potts, who was a clerk to the court at York.

Lister was, according to Potts, 'maliciously prosecuted by Master Lister'. Her trial had been in relation to the death of Thomas Lister senior, and young Thomas was convinced that Jennet had bewitched his father so much that he had died as a result. A servant had claimed that, as the older Thomas had died, he cried out 'in great extremity' that 'Preston's wife lays heavy upon me…help me, help me…' Both the servant and young Lister had testified that the dying man had ranted and raved when he thought that Jennet was in the house, saying, 'Look about for her and lay hold of her...For God's sake shut the door.'

They even said that, after death, Jennet touched the corpse and blood flowed.

On top of that, Roger Nowell from Lancashire sent more accusations; he claimed that Jennet, who had been married in Gisburn in 1587 and so was much older than Lister when she was supposedly his mistress, had been well treated by the Lister family and had been seen in her true colours of 'witch' when the new master took over. The most damning supposed evidence was that Jennet was said to have gone to a gathering (a coven) of witches at a place called Malkin Tower. Nowell had allegedly investigated this and reported that

LEMAN REDE, *YORK CASTLE*, 1829

Mary Bateman, 'The Yorkshire Witch', who was hanged at York in 1809.

Jennet and her peers had planned to 'put the said Master Thomas Lister of Westby to death, and after Master Lister should be taken away by witchcraft…'

But this all appears to be fabrication; historian Jonathan Lumby argues convincingly that Jennet was victimized by two powerful men. Potts wrote that she died on the scaffold 'impenitent and void of all fear or grace…she died an innocent woman because she would confess nothing'. The poor woman had been mercilessly victimized, the charges monopolizing on the general fears about demonology and the Pendle Witches story. After all, even the king, James I, had written a book on the subject, and that volume, called *Demonologie*, was clearly very influential concerning general myths and fears.

The other women convicted with her were destined to be holed up at Lancaster. They were tried at assize courts, and the outcome was that Anne Whittle, Alison Device, her son James, and seven others were condemned to die. They were not all executed, however, and historian Dick Hamilton points out that in 1636 ten of them were still in Lancaster prison, adding that 'One of them was Jennet Device, whose nine year old precocity had sent her mother to the stake…Some say there was too much local feeling for them to be set free. But the darkness of time has closed in on them forever.'

For most women in prison through the centuries, however, those who had committed the most common minor offences of larceny, abetting others, receiving or assisting in robberies, breaking and entering and so on, their destiny was hard work and a repressive regime. We know a great deal about the female convict prison at Brixton, for instance, from the documentary study by Mayhew and Binny in 1862. This prison had been built in 1820 and it was a tough place from the start. In 1854 the return of punishments administered to women included 288 sentences to the refractory cell, 92 on a bread and water diet, 31 in handcuffs, 34 confined to cell, and 246 deprived of a meal. The women's labour included work in the wash-house, the ironing room and needlework. Mayhew and Binny commented on the regimented discipline inside the walls:

As we passed down the different wards, examining the work as we went, each woman rose from her stool and curtseyed...One of the convicts was engaged in some delicate embroidery work. 'She's in for life' whispered one of the matrons...From seven till eight in the evening the same silence and work go on; but at this period the women sit within their cells and work.

Brixton also had a special convict nursery.

In the eighteenth century, as we know from a print by Hogarth called 'The harlot beating hemp', we have a scene from the Westminster bridewell in which several women prisoners are using massive wooden mallets to pound rolls of hemp into strands, and Hogarth shows the harshness of the regime by illustrating the stocks – and one woman is fastened into them, for failing to work hard enough. The stocks have the motto: 'Better to work than to stand thus'.

At that time, Howard also noticed, as in his visit to Liverpool bridewell in 1776, that the necessity of keeping women clean and free from lice and other pests sometimes went too far: '...the females [not the males] at their entrance, after a few questions, were placed, with a flannel shift on, and underwent a thorough ducking, thrice repeated – a use of a bath, which I dare say the legislature never thought of, when in their late Act they ordered baths with a view to cleanliness...not for the exercise of a wanton and dangerous kind of severity'. There is no doubt that keepers and warders derived a frisson of sadistic excitement in their treatment of women prisoners in some places.

As to numbers and the trajectory of prison life, a glance at some returns from the huge Millbank penitentiary gives some idea of this: in 1854 (January) there were 198 women prisoners, compared to 948 men. The women were disposed of as follows: 178 transferred to Brixton; 19 discharged, and one death.

Ten years later there were statistics issued for the whole prison establishment for England and Wales, and the average annual population was given as 129,527 (excluding debtors and those in military prisons). The reporter noted the sheer size of the criminal class: '...the average number in convict prisons was 8,055. These persons came from a criminal and suspected class estimated at above 150,000.' The female population was 34,487.

The *penal class* (longer sentences) rules for women at Millbank were:

1 To have their cells bolted up and be kept in strict separation.
2 To be engaged in picking coir or oakum for the first three months.
3 Not to be allowed to receive visits or letters.
4 Not to attend school for the first three months.
5 In the event of an offence against the rules, the governor shall have the power of punishing as laid down in rule 13, page 11 of the rules applicable to the governor.

Of course, there was a danger from another kind of mixing of women prisoners: the 'contamination' of younger and new offenders by the seasoned criminals. In Newgate, this was sorted out in 1818 when a documentary study of the prison was conducted by a Mr Bennett. He wrote that, 'In respect of the women prisoners, a great and important change for the better mode of confining them has taken place. They are not now the tried and untried mixed together; those under sentence of death are placed by themselves; but even here the convicts and fines (short-sentence women) are not separated. Girls of the tenderest years are associated with the most profligate characters.'

Bennett knew what Elizabeth Fry had achieved in that prison, and he noted that she and the Society of Friends had worked for the younger female offenders and 'placed this part of the prison in a state of comparative excellence'. They were dealing with ninety-seven women at that time, and one of the tried and convicted females was only eleven years of age. Bennett described what the place was like before these changes: 'The disgusting scenes that formerly occurred there have ceased…' He noted, though, that overcrowding was still a problem: 'But the system, even as it is, cannot be persevered in, and the benefits of this meagre and limited classification preserved if more not be given, for the numbers are not almost equal to the space allotted to them, and 170 women have been confined there at the same time.'

The Victorians were certain that there was a notable difference between male and female offenders. In 1862 a report expressed this with a sense of confidence: 'Women, it will be observed, are not very much more than a third of the men in number, but that women, when criminal, are worse than the men seems to be indicated by the fact that 42 in every 100 of the women in prison had been there the year before, but only 33 of the 100 in the men.' In 1872 a report on Irish convict prisons again made a special effort to mention the women: 'He regrets, too, that there are a few women in prison of violent, turbulent and incorrigible disposition, upon whom neither kindness, nor moral influence appears to have not the slightest effect.'

In the same year there was a meeting of the International Prison Congress, and Miss Carpenter gave a lecture on women prisoners. Her words concerned the female difference, with regard to crime, and she expresses the norm of the thinking then:

> In the course of her address she acknowledged that the women prisoners were, as a class, worse than the men, and she said it was better to state that openly than to hide it. One reason for this was that, as women were of a finer organization, when they broke down their fall was more complete than that of men, who might always look for rehabilitation whereas men would not.

She insisted that 'only the worst of the sex were in general in prison'.

Such attitudes were a contributory factor in convictions for murder, and particularly interesting are the cases involving wealthy, middle-class women convicted of serious crime. For instance, Florence Maybrick, wife to Liverpool businessman and Ripper suspect, James, was convicted of his murder. From her cell in Woking Invalid Convict prison, Florence Maybrick saw and carefully noted the best and the worst of the British penal system as it was at the end of the Victorian period. She had been moved there from Aylesbury prison, where she had been brought out of solitary confinement to be told that she was bound for a convict prison. In some ways that was a better place to be than a county prison, but for Florence, who had been used to a comfortable suburban middle-class life in Liverpool, and before that in America, this was disgusting and degrading. As we say today, with a tinge of cruel irony, welcome to jail, Madam. But first we have to explain how she came to be behind bars in 1889.

In the nineteenth century, the ubiquity of fly-papers in the average home was something that could lead from routine habits to a suggestion of heinous foul play. They were a neat way to rid the house of insects, but when they were soaked, for arsenic to be extracted for other uses, there could be trouble. In Battlecrease House, in Aigburth, this was a factor in the puzzling and desperately sad story of Florence Maybrick. To make matters worse for her, she was married to a man who enjoyed taking tiny quantities of poison, for all kinds of reasons.

When that man, James Maybrick, died, the finger of guilt pointed at his wife. The story went on to become not only a famous and controversial case, but a story that has been acquired by the vast library of Jack the Ripper theories, as James was in the habit of visiting London, and his strange personality gave rise to a certain line of enquiry about him.

The story of the Maybricks began when James was on board the liner *Baltic* in 1880. There he met young Florence, only eighteen at the time, though James was forty-two. Florence had been born in Mobile, Alabama; her mother aspired to wealth and status and wanted the same for her daughter. Florence's mother's third husband had been a German aristocrat, and so the American lady was actually no less than the Baroness von Roques if she wanted to pull rank or put on airs. James Maybrick, along with many other men, found Florence to be very alluring. She was an attractive blonde, blue-eyed and very shapely. It must have been a stunning contrast for her when they married and moved to Liverpool, after living first in Norfolk, Virginia, for a while.

After they married in 1881, they settled at Battlecrease House in Aigburth; this is a huge building, and Maybrick had acquired considerable wealth in the cotton business. But the change in lifestyle and cultural ambience must have been depressing for the young bride.

She was a product of the American South, and of the wealthy, social-izing element of that culture. Now she was in a British suburb of a fast-growing industrial city with a very sombre and grey climate. Society and social gatherings were limited for her, and her husband was often away from home.

They had children, and on the surface at least they would have appeared to be like every other middle-class couple. But the main problem lay with James. As time went by, his business foundered. Not only was he failing in commerce, but in his personality he was nurturing habits that would ruin his health. Maybrick was drawn to the questionable pleasures of taking poisons and drugs to keep an edge on life (in fact to enhance sexual potency, as arsenic was taken to do). He also lived the fairly typical double life of the Victorian married man: attentive husband at home but malcontented woman-izer when he could find the time and opportunity.

Clearly, Florence would soon find the stress of this relationship, and the loneliness it imposed on her, too much to handle. The fact that Maybrick then set about saving money at home by imposing privations and discipline on the domestic routine was perhaps the last straw. She wrote to her mother (living in Paris at the time) that she felt inclined to leave the house and move elsewhere, and doubted that 'life was worth living', because things were so bad. Her situation was ripe for the relief, pleasure and fulfilment that an affair would bring. She found the man in Alfred Brierley, a person in the same line of business as James.

Her mistake, as we look on her life with the knowledge of hind-sight, was that she was not discreet. She and Brierley would have times together in London posing as a married couple. But her strains at the hands of Maybrick were intolerable. He already had a mistress, and she became equally rash in her attempts to find pleasure outside marriage. There was an element of torment in their relationship, even to the point of Florence flirting with James's brother, Edwin. Things were moving towards some kind of crisis; they were not sleeping together, and Florence was thinking about leaving him.

At this point, enter the fly-papers. Because she was in the habit of using a mixture of arsenic and elderflower to treat boils on her face, the soaking papers were a common sight in the house. But then came James's illness. On 27 April, he was ill and he blamed this on a prescription of strychnine being wrongly calculated. This would have made sense of a man with those strange habits of pleasure. But his health began to decline more severely. Fate was stacking the odds against Florence, as the servants were noticing the soaking fly-papers and linking that to their master's decline. After all, he had cut her out of his will and had been insulting and aggressive towards her on many occasions. She had cause to detest him. The illness dragged on, and a nurse was employed to be with the patient at all times.

Maybrick's brother, Edwin, also arrived, and he took charge. The situation at the time was that Florence was estranged from her husband; she was seen as potentially a deranged woman with a grudge against him, and there was evidence mounting against her with regard to the arsenic. Even worse, bearing in mind the morality of the time, she wrote to her lover, Brierley, trying to arrange a meeting with him before he left the country; in that letter she referred to Maybrick's condition and noted that he had no suspicion of the affair. Florence was often present at the sick man's bedside and, unfortunately for her, she played a part in using the medicines, saying that James had actually asked her to give him some arsenic in powder form. Everything she seemed to do in the role of nurse or caring wife turned into facts to be used against her when Maybrick died, as he did on 11 May. She was arrested on suspicion of wilful murder by Superintendent Bryning.

The high drama continued even to the point of her mother entering the scene; there was a confrontation and Florence put the situation very succinctly, saying to her, 'They think I poisoned Jim.' She was taken first to Lark Lane station, and then to Walton prison.

The trial began at St George's Hall on 31 July, and Sir Charles Russell led her defence. There was great confusion in the forensic and medical evidence, even to the point of two experts disagreeing about whether or not the deceased had died from arsenic poisoning. Events went against her, and in the end it could be said that Florence was a victim of the judge. This is because there was just so much testimony about Maybrick's habits of pumping his body full of drugs and poisons that he was dicing with death anyway, and ruining his health for many years before these suspicions were first aroused about his wife's alleged designs on him. The judge, Mr Justice Fitzjames Stephen, directed his long summing-up to the likely guilt of Florence if certain facts were ignored: that is, he reinforced the accusations of moral lapses against her, to the detriment of the actual issue of murder. He was ludicrously biased in his dramatic account of the situation of slow poison on a supposed 'loved one'. Naturally, the jury would begin to turn against Florence and forget the contradictions about the actual nature and administering of the poison. Arguably, the judge's action that had the most impact on the jury was his mention of the letter to Brierley about Maybrick being 'sick unto death' and his very evident repugnance at what he was implying she had done and written with such callousness. The jury surely must have been influenced by seeing this. There was definitely 'reasonable doubt' in the case, and a death sentence was outrageous. Yet, on 7 August, Florence Maybrick was sentenced to hang. The judge, leaving the court, was the target of general public abuse and displeasure, so wrong was his sentence perceived to be.

The real heart of this sensational trial was Florence's loud assertion that she was innocent of this crime: 'I was guilty of intimacy with Mr Brierley, but I am not guilty of this crime.'

But the real sensation was yet to come – after the death sentence was passed on her. There was a strong and widespread campaign for clemency, and this was going on even at the time that Florence was waiting her fate in Walton prison (with gallows being made ready outside). The Home Secretary arranged a reprieve: the sentence was to be commuted to penal servitude for life. But in 1904 she was released and returned to America. There, as the writer Richard Whittington-Egan has stated, she hid herself away in the Berkshire foothills – becoming 'Florence Chandler' in South Kent, Connecticut. The person who became the epitome of the dotty and lonely old spinster, surrounded by cats, as Whittington-Egan says, 'was known to successive generations of South Kent boys as The Cat Woman'. She died in 1941, aged eighty-one. History tells of two Florence Maybricks, then, but there is another – the lonely prisoner, unjustly incarcerated, in those silent years before release.

History has leaned to the view that gastroenteritis, not murder, led to Maybrick's death.

In prison, Florence recorded everything and she wrote a book, *My Fifteen Lost Years*, after her release in 1904. This work gives us a tremendous amount of documentary information on life behind bars for women at that time. She expresses her condition in jail like this:

> Here I may state in general that I early found that thoughts of without and thoughts of within – those that haunted me of the world and those that were ever present in my surroundings – would not march together...the conflict between the two soon became unbearable...

She reflected that her 'safety' was in 'compressing her thoughts to the smallest compass of mental existence'. Florence is accurate and powerful in her account of the visiting time – something that is as stressful today as it always was. Her mother used to travel from France to see her, and the conditions they had at 'Visits' are described in Florence's book: 'Whenever my mother's visit was announced, accompanied by a matron I passed into a small oblong room. There a grilled screen confronted me; a yard or two beyond was a second barrier...and behind it I could see my mother...'

THE GRAPHIC, 1873

The press room: by the late Victorian period, the general public's curiosity about prison life was satisfied by the popular press. In this case, the visitor tries on the pinioning jacket.

Florence was the victim of something inherent in the prison system too – duped by another prisoner, using her for selfish means. The other prisoner gave her some fine wool for her stocking, after spilling hot water on her foot, and later there was a cell search (a 'spin') and the wool was found in her cell. She suffered greatly after that, as she wrote: 'I was degraded for a month to a lower stage, with a loss of twenty-six marks, and had six days added to my original sentence.'

In her own memoir of her life and prison existence, Florence left an account of the time she thought she was doomed:

> In all of the larger local English prisons there is one room, swept and ready, the sight of which cannot fail to stir unwanted thoughts. The room is large, with barred windows, and contains only a bed and a chair. It is the last shelter for those whom the law declares to have forfeited their lives. For nearly three weeks I was confined in this cell of the condemned to taste the bitterness of death.

One day the governor, Captain Anderson, came to the cell and said, 'Maybrick…no commutation of sentence has come down to me. It is my duty to tell you to prepare for your death.'

But in January 1904 she was released. Florence had always said that she bought the arsenic for use on fly-papers, ultimately to be used as a beauty treatment. After her death, among her few possessions people found a piece of paper on which was written the method of adapting fly-papers for cosmetic uses.

Now it is important to revisit the subject of 'child-murder' again, as it was responsible for so much suffering in the prison cells across the land for such a long time. As Clive Emsley has pointed out, 'Until 1803 the crime of infanticide was supposed to be tried under an Act of 1624 which defined the offence as one committed specifically by an unmarried woman.' But of course this was not maintained in its severity as time went by. Gradually, as the nineteenth century progressed, some increased understanding of puerperal insanity and depression related to childbirth gradually emerged. The change may be observed in the case of Eliza Higgins in 1857, who was tried for murder of her daughter at the Old Bailey, but was convicted of manslaughter as an act of mercy. By 1866 one lawyer observed that there was 'a great reluctance to hang women'.

But in the northern towns this state of affairs took rather longer to happen. At the heart of the issue was the crucially important need for a young woman to keep her good name, her position in society and her self-respect. This, naturally, had another undesirable side-effect: at times the affiliation orders after a bastard birth, demanding finance from putative fathers, meant that these men would sometimes run from the constraints and responsibilities, but would also be liable to encourage disposal of the child – surely a move seen as the easiest way out of all perceived problems. Under laws of 1733 and 1809, the unmarried mother simply had to name the supposed father and then the parish poor law personnel would move in. This fear was surely an inducement to find a murderous route out of problems. In 1852, for instance, Alfred Waddington of Sheffield killed his little daughter. He had been affiliated and 'he was ordered to pay two shillings a week for its support' but the *Annual Register* reported that 'The prisoner was in arrears in his payments for the support of the child and a summons was issued against him...' He killed the child with a shoe-maker's knife.

There was nothing new in all this: it is simply that long-standing problems were exacerbated by the new industrial conditions and urban growth. Children had always been either killed or abandoned and left to the parish. In 1638, for instance, a certain Ursula Harcourt of Carleton, as was reported in the quarter sessions records for the West Riding, '...is lately gone out of the country...and hath left behind her children which are already chargeable'. The churchwardens and overseers of the poor were left to sort it out.

The period in which there was the highest incidence of infanticide was the 1850s and 1860s. As Josephine McDonagh has put it, at that time 'Britain was stricken by an apparent epidemic of child murder'. A contemporary writer called Henry Humble, writing in 1866 about the epidemic, expressed the nature of the problem like this: 'Bundles are left lying about the streets, which people will not touch, lest the too familiar object – a dead body – should be revealed, perchance with a pitch plaster over its mouth or a woman's garter around its mouth.'

One typical example from Yorkshire happened at a railway station. In Wakefield a baby was born to one Annie Scruton, and she paid Mary Robson (of Bridlington) to adopt the child. The latter was one of a class of baby-farmers and she collected the baby, then waited for a train at Normanton; the problem was that the child was ill. In the early hours, the baby was dead, lying on a bench in the waiting room. At the inquest, as with so many of these sad cases, the blame was difficult to apportion. The result was that there was a verdict of neglect – not manslaughter, which would have been quite likely had there been a culprit to point at. This kind of infanticide happened everywhere, and there was very little in place in terms of social support for the mothers who could not cope with the expense of having a child to care for.

It was a Yorkshire-based doctor, Edmund Syson, who told the Select Committee looking into the problem that earlier in his career when he was a doctor near Rotherham, he had found out just how open a topic this was: 'I have been asked myself to kill a child as it was being born, and by a good-natured nurse too, and I'm sure she had no idea it was murder.' The historian Lionel Rose has explained the various methods used to 'kill off' unwanted babies. Obviously suffocation (lying on) was common, but also the vital organs could be punctured with needles, injuries to the head and neck could be put down to a difficult delivery, and at times a bucket was used so that the child could be drowned as soon as it emerged from the mother's body.

These attitudes may be seen in trials for infanticide or for 'concealing a birth' long after capital punishment for these offences had been abolished. There are some stories from the lives of young women who led precarious and uncertain lives in service, or drifting from job to job across Yorkshire, that create interest because they throw light on the human dilemmas that never go away. Some of these stories are tragic on a grand scale, whereas others are of a lower order, seedy and mundane. But there are also some of these tales that exist mainly as morality tales about the fallibility of human nature. In this category is the life of Maud Waines.

In August 1909, the *Bridlington Gazette* announced that in the local magistrates court there had been something very much out of the ordinary run-of-things in this sleepy seaside town: 'There are many details which are not fit for publication and it is only necessary to refer to the Chairman's suggestion that all respectable women, and respectable men too, should go out of the court, to indicate the nature of the case.' This brings to mind the famous saying about the British public in one of its fits of morality, as stated by Lord Macaulay: 'We know of no spectacle so ridiculous as the British public in one of its periodical fits of morality.' One would have thought that the *Bridlington Gazette* was trying to protect the sensibilities of a weak and gullible public.

What in fact was happening was that Maud Waine, a frail-looking girl of twenty-two who looked much younger, was in the dock on what was looking like a murder trial. It had all begun when, one morning in July 1909, a man called Stubbs, as he was walking on Sands Lane railway bridge in Bridlington, found a parcel in which the body of a baby was wrapped in linen. Good police work had tracked down the laundry numbers on the linen to the home of Mrs Crannis at 2 Marlborough Terrace in the town. It has to be said that the detective involved, Robson, did excellent work using the laundry numbers on towels and aprons. It needed close observation and attention to detail. What it did most of all was lead to Maud Waine, who was living in St John Street.

So began our knowledge of this sad, lonely young woman who had been led to a desperate act by her 'downfall', as seduction was expressed then. The indications for her future in the legal process were not good when it was noted that the police took away possessions from her, and these included a bottle of 'apioline', a substance of some importance later on. A Dr Forrest had examined the corpse of the infant and concluded that it had lived for some little time independently of the mother, so it was not a case of a stillbirth. He noticed a wound on its skull but this seemed to have been caused in the birthing period. Now Dr Forrest had to care for the mother in court, because Waine was constantly in poor health. She was of a weak constitution and needed constant attention, as the stresses of the proceedings were hard for her to bear.

Dr Forrest was called to her and she was always escorted, such was the concern. But despite all this, she stood in court and faced a charge of wilful murder. She pleaded not guilty and there was an adjournment. On remand, she had the care of the prison doctor in Hull, and he of course was expected to compile a report on her. Her lawyer, Mr Wray, had to make announcements on her delicate health and it became clear at the court when she next appeared that she had been more seriously ill in custody. Yet again the case was adjourned. This was guaranteed to interest the local press, as the murder charge, combined with the fascination of the woman's condition and frail presence in the dock, made this a good dramatic story.

At last the case was heard and her story was told. Waine had been in touch with a Hull man called Arnold Fisher and he had fixed a visit and a date with her while she was working in Beverley. But the *Gazette* reporter was in for a treat, when the detective Robson recounted a strange incident. He had been in a cab with Waine in Hull and as the cab stopped on Monument Bridge, the young woman had shrieked and pointed at a man passing by, saying it was Foster, and that he was the father of the dead child. She even knew that he worked at the Hull firm of the British Oil Mill Company.

It was then that the sad story emerged. Waine had been working in service, moving from post to post, and had met Foster in search of a little excitement. He had wooed her, courted her, and made promises of course; but she had been seduced and became pregnant. Luckily she had a friend and support in a woman called Louise Botterill in Bridlington, and she took care of the baby for the first six weeks until Waine found a position elsewhere. The long tale of misfortune gradually emerged: Waine had had the child, moved jobs, and then returned to Bridlington; there was no definite detail about the child and when and where she was seen with him around the date of the finding of the body. What was confirmed, though, was the medical evidence stating that the death had been due to a fall.

Waine had even been sacked from one place of employment due to her illness. Again, in the magistrates court, she fainted. Her precarious state of health in the dock made for high drama. Generally, the opinion was forming that she had not killed the child; evidence pointed to her love of children and her good nature. What was coming through as the truth here was that the child had died and she had held on to it for a while. The sympathy for her was now palpable and in court the bench decided that this was not a murder charge. Her lawyer in her defence made a plea for a much lesser charge to be applied. The outcome would happen at York assizes.

There, on 17 November, the charge Maud Waine faced was not murder, but merely concealment of birth. The presiding judge, Mr Justice Bucknill, a bencher of the Inner Temple, made it clear that this was not a murder case and said that the truth was that the girl had hidden the body of her child 'recently born'. The defence lawyer painted a sad picture of the woman giving birth while unconscious, and that the child had had the fall. Most likely, it had survived a few months but died of injuries sustained at the time of the fall. There were plenty of good things said about Waine's character, and the most astonishing sidelight we have on her true nature from all this is how tough she was, in spite of ill health, and also that she was driven to desperation by the stigma of illegitimate birth. She had suffered in silence and not told her Burton Agnes family, going through the demands of the pregnancy alone.

The result was a binding over and a fine of £5. We have to point the finger of blame at the man from Hull, as indeed Bucknill did. But there was nothing to be done in that quarter. Overall, the tale of Maud Waine is one of its time: a saga of public shame and inner humiliation, all from a desire to have some fun and break the monotony of life in service.

Also relevant in this context, with young women and children in mind, is the arrival of the reformatory. The idea that young offenders should have more than a prison sentence and hard labour took some shifting, but when Mary Carpenter of Bristol came along and realized that for reclamation of young women from their criminal lives to take place, approaches other than penal measures would soon be needed. She saw that young female prisoners would soon learn more criminal behaviour if placed with older women in a prison.

In 1851 she published an essay, 'Reformatory Schools for the

Children of the Perishing and Dangerous Classes and for Juvenile Offenders'. A conference followed on juvenile offenders, and then established the Red Lodge reformatory on Park Row in Bristol. Her principles were based on love and affection, with as much individual care as possible; she also thought that small scale was best, because a reformatory that could be something akin to a family would be more likely to succeed in rehabilitation of the girls. But, of course, the child also had to agree to change, so co-operation was needed. This did not always work out as Mary Carpenter might have desired, and in fact in the basement of the Red Lodge there were cells. Reformatories were a kind of prison in some ways, but the cells were a last resort.

Typical of the girls at Red Lodge might have been eleven-year-old Julia Osgothorpe, born in Nottingham, who stole some bread and was sentenced to fourteen days in prison and five years in a reformatory; she went to Red Lodge. There is a photograph of her, and it shows a frail little girl, just 4 feet 1 inch tall, looking almost angelic. The impression one has is that this particular inmate would respond to affection and close guidance. But it would always be a gamble. After all, the regime in the reformatory was based on the redemptive qualities of work and Christian worship, with firm discipline. Not all girls would welcome that.

Carpenter was eminently sensible and open-minded, writing that 'Each case should be dealt with on its merits, release dependent on progress made, and decided by the school managers under a government inspection.' The most positive point to make about her school, though, was that there was no corporal punishment there. Even in confinement, there was one-to-one reasoning and an optimism that a good change would come about in the individual.

Gradually, women who had been suffering, in modern terms, from 'postnatal depression' or even 'postnatal psychosis' were looked at with more understanding by the penal system, so that more were sent to reformatories or asylums towards the end of the nineteenth century. By the 1870s there were the beginnings of more specialist areas of psychology, and the 'alienists', as they were called then, began to understand more about the effects on a woman's mental health of childbirth – particularly in those social contexts in which there was extreme poverty and deprivation.

As these matters progressed and more enlightened ideas on sentences emerged, women's penal destinations were often the asylum rather than the prison cell.

In February 1923 Mrs Grace Castle put her three children in the bath at her home in Market Place. As if possessed and driven by an inner voice, she forced their heads under the water and drowned them. The three children, the oldest only seven, were found just before midnight that night when police arrived. It has to have been one of the most tragic events in the chronicles of Yorkshire murder. In fact, the very word 'murder' is paradoxically unfitting. Poor Grace Castle was in need of help; her mind was deranged and she had allowed a terrible voice of unreason and destruction to creep into her being.

On that horrendous evening, she had tried to ring her husband Fred, who was at a Freemasons' meeting. But there had been no telephone there. Circumstances conspired that evening to lead the woman to kill. Her husband was a good man, and had fought in the Great War, coming home to work as a brewer's manager at Market Place. He had also been a well-known local footballer, playing for Driffield and for Cranswick. Not only did she kill her sons, but she tried to take her own life as well, taking a tincture of iodine. The poignant situation here was that in her mind she had killed the family 'for him'.

When the police officer arrived, Grace Castle was sitting in the kitchen in a state of mental turmoil, saying, 'Oh Mr Waind, you don't know why I have done it!' Why she had done it is difficult to explain but her own words are given on a piece in her notebook:

Whatever happens don't spend a penny on me. I am cursed and so are my children. The only way I was to have saved their souls was to have killed them…Now I cannot see a way out at all. My husband is the best father and a fine man. He worships his children and what a disappointment for him to have seen them grow up in desperation and crime…

An insight into her condition was provided by the maid in the house, Alice Harper, who was with Mrs Castle earlier that evening. She said that the children were put to bed about 7.45 p.m., but that when they were asleep, Grace was in pain. Alice thought she was suffering from her usual neuralgia. Ultimately everyone managed to get to bed, but Alice was roused from her sleep at 11.30 when she found Grace sitting in the kitchen saying that her head felt funny and then said, 'Oh my poor bairns!'

The first meeting of the coroner's inquest was a brief affair and was adjourned. Thomas Holtby, the coroner, summed up the feeling at the time when he said that the deaths constituted the 'saddest tragedy' he had ever come across. The inquest was adjourned until medical evidence was available. The Reverend George Storer presided at the funeral of the children. Grace Castle was charged with murder, having malice aforethought, and of course was guilty of attempted suicide as well.

Then, at the resumed inquest, some medical evidence came from the family doctor, Dr Keith, a man who had fought alongside Fred Castle in the war. He confirmed that Grace had suffered from some kind of nervous condition for six months; Keith had attended on the night of the deaths and there he found that she had presumably taken the iodine simply because it was something 'chemical', as it was hardly the type of substance a person would take if they wanted to die quickly. All she could say was that the doctor would see from her writings why she had done it. She was totally distracted and, although aware of what she had done and how she had killed, it was all somehow unreal to her, outside her range of comprehension.

She was detained in Hull prison awaiting her trial, and at this point the journalists had begun to be annoyingly insensitive and intrusive, so much so that a member of the jury requested that he make a statement on this, saying that he wished to express strong disapproval of the flash-lights and cameras being used. Through modern eyes, there is nothing unusual or unexpected in this, but in 1923 the moral universe was more rigid and, especially in the quieter areas in the provinces, a 'big story' in the eyes of a journalist out to make a name for himself was far more than that – it was a terrible local sadness.

At York assizes in March, Dr Howlett, the prison doctor in Hull, was called to give an assessment of Grace's condition. He confirmed what Dr Simpson, the medical superintendent of the East Riding, had said – that though she could put into words the sequence of events on that tragic night, she was unable to feel any impression of emotion or derive meaning from this. Consequently both medical men agreed that she was insane. In fact, Simpson noted that it was a case of 'long-standing insanity'.

Her youngest son, Kenneth, had been only three, and it was noted during the investigation that Grace Castle had been 'in a poor state of health' since Kenneth's birth. For clues as to why she chose to kill in this way and for the reasons given, we can theorize that partly her motives were altruistic – thinking that the one she loved would be better off for the lack of stress caused by worry about the children, and also that her own problems (depression) would be alleviated. The tincture of opium is an interesting detail, because it bears no relation to any substance used commonly in these contexts: using tincture of opium bears the hallmark of desperation and irrational thought. It also seems highly likely that Grace Castle was suffering from postnatal depression and, in the circumstances in which she had to live, little was done to address this. The spirit of the times was to press on regardless. Even with a maid and help around the house, Grace was still under pressure, and it was from a deep well of unhappiness within her.

Grace Castle was therefore unfit to plead and was admitted to Broadmoor on 9 March 1923. The historian Helen Stewart has tried to follow up the future course of the parents' lives, but little has emerged. A man who went to the funeral of the children recalled that Fred Castle had been ill in later life, and had remained a Freemason, but as to Grace, we know nothing of her later life and her ultimate fate remains a mystery.

Women in prisons through the ages, then, have been extremely negatively defined and explained, with very little in the way of sociological elements in attempts to understand their situation and their essential difference as individuals within the great processes of social change that affected all lives from the Industrial Revolution onwards.

In 2007, Baroness Corston argued, in her report on women in prisons in the twenty-first century, that none of them should be there: that other, alternative sentences should be given. The debate goes on. For several centuries, there were no prisons dedicated specifically for women; their criminality, as has been stressed previously, was seen as far more extreme, against 'nature' and to be condemned far more than crimes committed by men. Even today, the tabloids often express a similar bias, differentiating between male and female offences in ways that reinforce prejudicial thought. At least we are now aware of the disastrous consequences on family stability of women being incarcerated, but radical changes are still needed.

Conclusions

The history of prisons in British social history, as I have shown, is something that clearly supports the view that one may consider how civilized a state is by the conditions under which its prisoners live. In the first recorded prisons, there was no system, but merely an *ad hoc* provision, later becoming a matter of business as prisons were franchised, run by the Church or by barons. Then the local prisons emerged and the problems that were to run deeply through the centuries were established there: payment of turnkeys, bribery and corruption and exploitation of the weak inside the walls.

Later came the emergence of prisons for all kinds of purposes, and in cities the prison provision became something so prominent that, by the Georgian years, debtors' prisons in London, for instance, became institutions that were not wholly places of dungeons and oblivion. Debtors in the King's Bench, for instance, could come out into the streets for part of the day, a curfew being imposed. The King's Bench prison was destroyed in 1780 by the destruction brought about by the Gordon Riots, and it was a grim landmark to all Londoners, having been there in Southwark, to the east of Borough High Street, less than a mile from London Bridge, since the fourteenth century. The conditions inside always depended on what prisoners could gather by way of finances, but in 1754 reports had shown what an awful place it was, but by the early nineteenth century it was noted as a place where, if a small fee was paid, a prisoner could even be allowed to leave for a day or two. William Combe, a hack writer, was allowed to live in the 'Liberties' – the area outside a borough where traditionally freemen held customary rights. In an interesting sidelight on life in the Bench around 1800, Henry Angelo wrote in his memoirs of visiting a friend there, 'In the Bench…everybody knows that there is plenty of space to play at racket, which serves for an amusement as well as to improve the health. Often we mounted the top of the prison there…secure from being seen, and we played with the Highland broadswords.'

Combe, because he still had work, had a small income. The idea was that creditors would wait until their debtor's circumstances changed and payments could be made to them. Obviously, if the debtor was thrown into a dark room and forgotten then nothing would ever be received from them. The debts Combe had were largely from Stephen Casey, the owner of the asylum in Plaistow where Combe's wife had been for years. But also he had been taking a small pension and that had been withdrawn, and the printers he worked for, Boydells, were in straitened circumstances. They had been paying him a retainer and that had to be reduced. As if all this were not enough, he had lived beyond his means. In 1790 he was living the life of an urban gentleman with a horse and servant, and as he loved the harpsichord, he bought a new one at the time, but on credit. By the late 1790s all these pressed on him. He had even owed cash to the painter George Romney, and we know that Combe wrote to Romney in 1798:

My dear Sir,

I have called several times in Cavendish Square, & you were always at your villa – I have frequently designed to see you there in your rustic glory, but my engagements and the shortness of the days have prevented my enjoying that pleasure – It will not, however, be long before I shall take the opportunity to wait upon you, and to repay the obligation you were so very good as to confer upon your faithful and obliged humble servant.

Wm Combe.

This is clearly the voice of a man accustomed to the required ruses and excuses of a situation of severe debt; it is also from a man who lives on the edge of order and rationality.

On 4 May 1799 the bailiff called and a week or so later he stood in the court of King's Bench; two men called Douglas and Lambert were suing for the sum of £40 11s 6d.

Combe had some experience studying law and so had no attorney. He lost, and so began a second term in prison. Stephen Casey was pursuing him for a vast sum of almost £200 without costs.

In the King's Bench he lived well, though. He was not a common debtor: he could eat and drink well. Tradesmen came into the prison each morning with food and materials; he would not have had to share a cell ('chum up' as it was called); the artists Rowlandson and Pugin drew the Bench prison in the 'Microcosm of London' in 1809, showing the large panoramic sweep of its interior open ground and the throngs of people walking and talking, behind them the high walls and the blocks, constructed along the lines of what would be the new penitentiaries.

The case of Combe shows just how much at that time prison could be a part of the community in many ways, with traders being allowed inside, and keepers making profits from inmates. In contrast, prisons today are mainly out of town centres, and citizens do not stop to think about the community in their midst. To enter prison is to lose one's identity and step into a limbo where the concept of the familiar self slips away and time blurs into one endless period of sameness. Yet hundreds of staff work in these prisons; to them, administration and supervision are merely days of normal work.

The most massive and remarkable difference between the Georgians and Stuarts and how they saw prison and ourselves today is of course the provision for care and education inside the prison community. Now we provide courses, a health service and, more recently, drama workshops, choirs and tuition in the visual arts.

In 2010, the dominant ideology is that prison may not work, but it is as a punishment, not for a punishment. Huge sums of money are spent with the belief that rehabilitation is possible, and the coalition government of 2010 is searching for ways to reduce the prison population, which stands at 86,000 as I write this. The cost of maintaining a person in prison at this time is almost £40,000 per annum.

In 1710, the concept of a prison was that it was a workhouse under another name, and when workhouses were conceived by the Elizabethans, there was little difference between that institution and the bridewell. Not until the 1850s did notions of rehabilitation and reform really set in.

We keep on asking what prison is for and whether or not it works, yet two facts have remained constant in the answers to those questions: first, the public are protected from dangerous people when the menace is contained in a prison and, second, as was written on the walls of York Castle female penitentiary in 1780, a prison is very much a 'house of care' as well as a place of deprivation and loss of freedom. That paradox has always been there in every historical context.

Those who have conceived and established prisons, from the first hellish pits and cages where torture and deprivation crushed the prisoner, have understood that the prison has to work by extreme suppression or by the exercise of what we would now call the psychology of group dynamics, but what was formerly conceived of as a hierarchy of power, cowing the dehumanized victim of the system.

At the heart of this thinking about what makes a working and successful prison is the erasure of identity. Even today, the new arrival at a prison enters 'reception' and that entails a relentless and minutely planned depersonalization. A person walks into the reception gate wearing his normal clothes and with pockets and possessions. After what the American language refers to as 'being processed', he is a non-person, an entity with a number and a regulation set of clothing. His possessions have been placed in a labelled bag, along with his civilian clothing, until he is released. The prisoner has stepped into an alternative world: a place in which time is ordered differently and, in a sense, stops, loses real meaning, as the days coalesce into months and the months into years. When Oscar Wilde entered Pentonville prison in 1895 he was transmuted into the fashion-loving, stylish writer and wit into a piece of government property – wearing the suit of black arrows to signify that fact, and Wilde has written of that first impact of 'being inside':

> The first evening they made me undress before them and get into some filthy water they called a bath and dry myself with a damp brown rag…The cell was appalling; I could hardly breathe and the food turned my stomach…I did not eat anything for days and days…as soon as I ate anything it produced violent diarrhoea and I was ill all day and night.

The uniform of the officers who control and regulate has also been, in most cases, very much a powerful symbolic element of control. In the first dungeons and prisons, these professions would have been military or related to the livery of a specific lord and master. As time went by, the dress was entirely militaristic; today it is relentlessly black and white in Britain, with a universal attire of white shirt and epaulettes, black trousers and shoes, and a buttoned, police-style jacket again in black. The officers are ranked as in a military structure, and there are officers of a lower status in the hierarchy known as 'OSGs' – Officer Support Grade.

The prison has always had an ambiguous status too: it was always conceived as a version of limbo, because it was a community outside the 'normal' community of citizens. Inmates are deprived of citizenship in most places; they become non-persons. It is easy to see why so much prison literature has reached for metaphors of a spiritual nature. Dante's circles of *The Divine Comedy* have a purgatory in which spirits trapped in non-time express the pain of their static condition, existing in a shadowland created by someone else. Being a community with its own rules, a prison in the years of Empire was just as subject to extreme punishment without check or compassion if those in command were bloody-minded and out to teach a lesson. Offences come and go, but in 1805 when sedition was a fearful thought for those in command, this could happen: 'On Thursday a private received 400 lashes in the Horse Barracks-yard at Ipswich, for uttering seditious expressions in a public house in the neighbourhood. Detachments from all the regiments in the garrison were present at the punishment.' In other words, punishment was a deterrent, and more extremely so in times of general peril or external threat. Prisons were seen as places in which that attitude could be applied against those incarcerated, and often without redress.

The massive corpus of prison literature provides my narrative with reminders of the fundamental facts of what a prison is, essentially, regardless of where or when it was established. This writing constantly expresses the see-saw interplay of punishment and redemption. Prison has always been a place and a concept of spiritual activity and thought; the very word 'cell' suggests a monkish life of course, and prisons from the early modern period to the present day have had chapels and chaplains. Since the modern prisons in Europe around the late seventeenth century, and even in the first bridewells of the Elizabethan years, there has been an acknowledgement that a criminal incarcerated is in need of knowledge of potential redemption.

In 1976 the old building of Holloway prison was demolished, and on the foundation stone (still preserved in the new prison) are these words from 1849: 'May God preserve the City of London, and make this place a terror to evil-doers.'

The thinking behind that has been at the very centre of penology in Britain since prisons were first conceived as a part of the social fabric and of the criminal justice system. The gradual transmutation from places in which a massive criminal underclass was contained and forgotten to a community with caring and individual help and guidance was a painful process, and a great learning experience for the staff. Today, officers and inmates meet to have meetings on individual 'sentence planning' and yet only within the last fifteen years have such unwholesome tasks as 'slopping out' the cell and urinating into buckets ceased in prisons.

Looking at the history of British prisons, is it tempting to say that we, as a nation, had a penchant for inflicting pain. Yet some of the most harrowing tales from penal chronicles have come from times in which the chattering classes debated endlessly on 'enlightened' and 'reformist' ideas. From the time that the reformers Howard, Fry, Romney and Wilberforce opened up prisons for scrutiny and malpractice for admonishment and disgust, there was a creeping, stealthy acceptance that perhaps we had our own 'slaves' here at the core of the Empire, as well as within the colonies and work-camps across the oceans.

One inescapable conclusion is that progress and change, as in so many things in society, were largely *ad hoc*, or simply made by pragmatic decisions. Policies came and went and recommendations from enquiries and commissions were often ignored. Even legislation was often ignored, notably in the Regency years. The House of Correction Act of 1784 made all the right legislative statements, but enforcement was beyond the scope and capabilities of the government. Only with the consolidation of the office and actions of the Home Secretary did matters improve. Surely Sir Robert Peel was one of the key figures in the whole of prison history, and a fitting reference to end this survey with is his achievement in his Gaol Act of 1823. As his biographer Douglas Hurd summarized:

> The Gaol Act of 1823 proposed a system of classification. It forbade the use of alcohol in prison and called for the appointment of a surgeon and a chaplain. Education was to be provided, and magistrates were required to inspect prisons regularly. The outline of our modern prison system began to emerge...

Bibliography

Books

Note: These are all editions used for reference, and not necessarily first editions of primary sources. The sources for prison history are diverse, and often some of the best information is to be found in memoirs and enquiries, but in recent years there has been a flowering of substantial surveys, particularly of the London prisons, and these include discussions of classic contemporary texts. There has also been a burgeoning of local monographs in recent years, and this local knowledge often comprises massive collections of statistics regarding prisons.

Family history study has also unearthed much more information about local prisons and their inmates. Magazines such as *Family History Monthly* and *Your Family Tree* often cover such topics.

Anyone wanting a concise overview of prison life should consult (a) the research guides on the National Archives website, and (b) the explanatory pages on prisons on the Old Bailey Sessions papers online (see below):

Abbott, Geoffrey, *Lipstick on the Noose* (Summersdale, 2003).

Abbott, Geoffrey, *Execution* (Summersdale, 2005).

Anon., *Genuine Account of the Life of John Rann, Alias Sixteen-String Jack* (Bailey printers, 1774).

Anon., *Fifty Amazing Hairbreadth Escapes* (Odhams, 1920).

Anon., *The Strangeways Murder* (Sporting News, Manchester, 1870). Reprinted by Clifford Elmer Books in 2004.

Anon., *Cries from the Past: A History of Lincoln Castle Prison* (Lincolnshire County Council, 2007).

Arnold, Catherine, *Bedlam: London and its Mad* (Pocket Books, 2008).

Bamford, Samuel, *Passages in the Life of a Radical* (OUP, 1994).

Birkenhead, Earl of, *Famous Trials* (Hutchinson, 1925).

Bland, James, *The Common Hangman* (Zeon Books, 1984).

Burnley, James, *West Riding Sketches* (Hodder & Stoughton, 1875).

Byrne, Richard, *Prisons and Punishment in London* (Harrap, 1989).

Calder, Angus, *Gods, Mongrels and Demons* (Bloomsbury, 2003).

Carey, Tim, *Mountjoy, The Story of a Prison* (Collins Press, 2000).

Cooper, T. P., *The History of the Castle of York* (Elliot Stock, 1911).

Coyle, Andrew, *Understanding Prisons* (OUP, 2005).

Cyriax, Oliver, *The Penguin Dictionary of Crime* (Penguin, 2000).

Davies, Mark, *Stories of Oxford Castle* (Oxford Towpath, 2008).

Dixon, C. W., *Mary and Caroline and the Lay Contribution to Preventive Medicine* (University of Otago Press, 1961).

Evans, Stewart P., *Executioner: The Chronicles of James Berry* (Sutton, 2004).

Foucault, Michel, *Discipline and Punish* (Penguin, 1977).

French, Yvonne (ed.), *News from the Past 1805–1887* (Gollancz, 1940).

Friar, Stephen, *The Sutton Companion to Local History* (Sutton, 2001).

Geltner, G., *The Medieval Prison: A Social History* (Princeton University Press, 2008).

Godfrey, Barry and Lawrence, Paul, *Crime and Justice 1750–1950* (Willan, 2005).

Gray, Adrian, *Crime and Punishment in Victorian Lincolnshire* (Paul Watkins, 1993).

Gregory, Jeremy, and Stevenson, John, *Britain in the Eighteenth Century* (Routledge, 2007).

Griffiths, Arthur, *Secrets of the Prison-House* (Chapman and Hall, 1894).

Grovier, Kelly, *The Prison: The Story of Newgate* (John Murray, 2008).

Halliday, Stephen, *Newgate: London's Prototype of Hell* (Sutton, 2006).

Harrison, Richard, *Foul Deeds Will Rise* (John Long, 1958).

Hawkes, Jean (ed. and translator), *The London Journal of Flora Tristan* (Virago, 1982).

Herber, Mark, *Legal London* (Phillimore, 1999).

Hibbert, Christopher, *The Roots of Evil: A Social History of Crime and Punishment* (Sutton, 2003).

Honeybone, Michael, *Wicked Practise and Sorcerye* (Baron Buckingham, 2008).

Howard, D. L., *John Howard, Prison Reformer* (Christopher Johnson, 1955).

Howard, John, *The State of the Prisons* (Everyman, 1920).

Hudson, Roger, *Hudson's English History* (Weidenfeld & Nicolson, 2005).

Hurd, Douglas, *Robert Peel: A Biography* (Weidenfeld & Nicolson, 2005).

Huxley, Ann, *Four Against the Bank of England* (John Long, 1969).

Irving, Ronald, *The Law is an Ass* (Duckworth, 1999).

Jackson, Lee, *A Dictionary of Victorian London* (Anthem, 2006).

Jackson, Stanley, *The Old Bailey* (W H Allen, 1978).

James, Trevor, *About Dartmoor Prison* (Hedgerow Print, 2001).

Jones, Dan, *Summer of Blood* (Harper Press, 2009).

Jones, Steve, *Yorkshire: The Sinister Side* (Wicked Books, 2004).

Kilday, Anne-Marie, and Nash, David, *Histories of Crime: Britain 1600–2000* (Macmillan, 2010).

Knipe, William, *Tyburn Tales: The Criminal Chronology of York Castle* (Burdekin, 1867).

Lee, John, *John Babbacombe Lee, The Man They Could Not Hang* (Devon Books, 1985).

Leech, Mark (ed.), *The Prisons Handbook* (Waterside Press, annual).

Linebaugh, Peter, *The London Hanged* (Verso, 2003).

Linnane, Fergus, *The Encyclopaedia of London Crime and Vice* (Sutton, 2003).

Low, Donald, *The Regency Underworld* (Sutton, 2005).

Lytton, Constance, *Prisons and Prisoners* (Virago, 1988).

Mayhew, Henry, and Binny, John, *The Criminal Prisons of London* (Griffin, Bohn, 1862).

Melling, Elizabeth, *Kentish Sources VI Crime and Punishment* (Kent County Council, 1969).

Montaigne, Michel de, *On Solitude* (Penguin Great Ideas, 2009).

Morris, Norval *et al.*, *The Oxford History of the Prison* (OUP, 1998).

Partridge, Col. S. G., *Prisoner's Progress* (Hutchinson, 1910).

Pocock, Sally J., *Behind Bars: A Chronicle of Bodmin Prison* (author publication, 2005).

Priestley, Philip, *Victorian Prison Lives* (Pimlico, 1999).

Pugh, Ralph B., *Imprisonment in Medieval England* (Cambridge University Press, 2008).

Rede, Thomas Leman, *York Castle* (Saunders, 1829).

Rees, Sian, *The Floating Brothel* (Review, 2001).

Richardson, John, *The Local Historian's Encyclopaedia* (Historical Publications, 1972).

Rolph, C. H., *The Queen's Pardon* (Cassell, 1978).

Ruggles-Brise, E., *The English Prison System* (Macmillan, 1921).

Saul, Nigel, *A Companion to Medieval England 1066–1485* (Tempus, 2005).

Saunders, John B., *Mozley and Whiteley's Law Dictionary* (Butterworths, 1977).

Seddon, Peter, *The Law's Strangest Cases* (Robinson, 2005).

Sharpe, James, *Crime in Early Modern England 1550–1750* (Longman, 1999).

Sharpe, James, *Dick Turpin: The Myth of the English Highwayman* (Profile, 2004).

Spargo, Tamsin, *Wanted Man* (Bloomsbury, 2005).

Stokes, Anthony, *Pit of Shame: The Real Ballad of Reading Prison* (Waterside, 2007).

Thomas, Donald, *State Trials* (Routledge & Kegan Paul, 1972).

Thomas, J. E., *The English Prison Officer Since 1850* (Routledge & Kegan Paul, 1972).

Wade, Stephen, *House of Care* (Bar None Books, 2007).

Wade, Stephen, *Britain's Most Notorious Prisoners* (Pen and Sword, 2010).

Wade, Stephen, *Thomas Rowlandson* (Amberley, 2010).

Wiener, Martin, *Reconstructing the Criminal: Culture, Law and Policy in England 1830–1914* (Cambridge University Press, 1990).

Wiener, Martin, *Men of Blood: Violence, Manliness and Criminal Justice in Victorian England* (Cambridge, 2004).

Younghusband, Sir George, *The Tower of London* (Herbert Jenkins, 1930).

Articles in journals/on the internet

Argent, Valerie,'Counter-Revolutionary Panic and the Treatment of the Insane' at http://stydymore.org.uk/1800.htm.

Brown, Alyson, 'Mutinies in Chatham Convict Prison 1861 and Dartmoor Convict Prison 1932', *Prison Service Journal*, vol. 166, pp. 45–9.

Cockburn, J. S., 'Seventeenth Century Clerks of Assize – Some Anonymous Members of The Legal Profession', *The American Journal of Legal History*, vol. 13, no. 4 (October 1969), pp. 315–32.

Cooper, Robert Alan, 'Ideas and Their Execution: English Prison Reform', *Eighteenth Century Studies*, vol. 10, no.1, 1976, pp. 73–93.

Dalrymple, Theodore, 'Inside Stories', *British Medical Journal*, 2009, p. 338.

Dooley, Enda, 'Unnatural Deaths in Prison', *British Journal of Criminology*, 1990, pp. 229–34.

Kane, Jacqueline L., 'Prison Palace or "Hell upon Earth": Leicester County Prison Under the Separate System, 1846–1865', *Transactions of the Leicestershire Archaeological and Historical Society*, LXX, 1996, pp. 128–46.

Keneally, Thomas, 'Convict Nation', *BBC History Magazine*, July 2006, pp. 35–40.

Neild, J., 'Mr Neilds' Remarks on Prisons', *Gentleman's Magazine*, 1805.

Redfern, Barry, 'Crime and Punishment in the 18th Century', *Family and Local History Handbook*, vol. 9, 2007, pp. 102–4.

Smith, Peter Scharf, 'Solitary Confinement', *Prison Service Journal*, January 2009, no. 181, pp. 3–11.

White, Jerry, 'Pain and Degradation in Georgian London: Life in the Marshalsea Prison', *History Workshop Journal* 68, 2009, pp. 69–98.

Woodfine, Philip, 'Debtors, Prisons and Petitions in Eighteenth Century England', *Eighteenth Century Life*, vol. 30, no. 2, Spring 2006, pp. 1–31.

Websites

www.blacksheepindex.org
www.british-history.ac.uk
www.capitalpunishmentuk.org
www.corpun.com/uk
www.infed.org/thinkers/carpenter.htm
www.learningcurve.gov.uk
www.luminarium.org
www.oldbaileyonline.org
www.staffordshire.go.uk
www.tipp.ie/butlerca.htm
www.victorianweb.org

Newspapers and journals consulted

Annual Register
Daily Telegraph
Freeman's Journal
Gentleman's Magazine
Hobarton Mercury
Hull Packet
Illustrated Police News
Legal History
Notes and Queries
Observer
Prison Service Journal
St James's Chronicle
Social History
The Graphic
Times Digital Archive

Archives and official sources

British Parliamentary Papers
Hansard: 1821
London Metropolitan Archives: Coroner's Records: information leaflet 34
Report of the Committee of the Society for the Improvement of Prison Discipline (T. Bensley, 1820)
Report on Prison Dietaries (HMSO, 1899)

Museums

The Clink Prison Museum: www.clink.co.uk
Dartmoor Prison and Visitor Centre: www.dartmoor-prison.co.uk
www.galleriesofjustice.org.uk
Hexham: The Old Prison at Hexham:
www.tynedaleheritage.org/Resources/Prison
Parkhurst Prison Heritage Museum: www.wightonline.co.uk
www.riponmuseums.co.uk
Tolbooth Prison Museum, Aberdeen: wwwaboutaberdeen.com/toll-booth
www.yorkcastlemuseum.org (the York Dungeons experience)

INDEX